Albert Ross Parsons

Parsifal

The finding of Christ through art or, Richard Wagner as theologian

Albert Ross Parsons

Parsifal

The finding of Christ through art or, Richard Wagner as theologian

ISBN/EAN: 9783744758703

Printed in Europe, USA, Canada, Australia, Japan

Cover: Foto ©ninafisch / pixelio.de

More available books at **www.hansebooks.com**

PARSIFAL

THE FINDING OF CHRIST THROUGH ART

OR

RICHARD WAGNER AS THEOLOGIAN

BY

ALBERT ROSS PARSONS

PRESIDENT OF THE MUSIC TEACHERS' NATIONAL ASSOCIATION

———

" The God revealed to us by Jesus—this God who never can be revealed again, because then and for the first time he was revealed to mankind."—RICHARD WAGNER.

NEW YORK & LONDON

G. P. PUTNAM'S SONS

The Knickerbocker Press

1890

The Knickerbocker Press, New York
Electrotyped, Printed, and Bound by
G. P. Putnam's Sons

PREFACE.

THE main text of the present work is substantially identical with a lecture entitled "The Finding of Christ through Art; or, Richard Wagner as Theologian," delivered before the Lecture Chapter of the Guild of All Souls Church (Episcopal), New York City, Sunday afternoon, May 19, 1889, by invitation of the Guild, through the Rev. R. Heber Newton, D.D., rector of the parish.

As the time at the lecturer's command upon such an occasion would not admit of an exhaustive presentation of the evolution and final outcome of Wagner's thoughts upon religion during a period of forty years, the matter chosen and the form of the lecture were determined by the circumstances of the occasion, including the time and place of its delivery and the audience which was likely to assemble to hear it.

In preparing it for publication, the determining circumstances connected with the occasion of its first public reading lose their importance, and it becomes a duty to extend its dimensions and add to its material in ways which a regard to the larger circle of the reading community would naturally suggest. In the present edition of this lecture, the additional material is presented mainly in the form of notes and appendices.

Of writing many books on the story and the musical and dramatic workmanship of Wagner's music-dramas there is no end, and in this interpretative labor the Parsifal is by no means being neglected. In the present work we are to consider the master's creation from quite another point of view. We are not to ask *what* Wagner wrote in Parsifal, nor *how* he wrote it, musically and otherwise, but instead, how he came to write the work at all. Or, in other words, we are to inquire what sort of a personal relation to, and what sort of an interest in, Christianity it was which impelled him to the toil involved in the design and execution of such a work, and which caused his genius to glow with the sublime devotional and emotional inspirations which characterize this, the Swan's Song of his astonishing artistic career.

By some, Wagner has been deemed a Buddhist, and not without a show of reason; for his study of Schopenhauer would naturally lead to more or less familiarity with the principles of Hindu religion. Indeed, in Parsifal, in the scene in Klingsor's garden, in which we are reminded of the apostolic expression, "in all points tempted like as we are yet without sin," to meet the requirements of dramatic art, Wagner obviously turns to the legend of Buddha's temptation by the daughters of Mara disguised as beautiful women. But the words quoted on our title-page would seem to show conclusively that Wagner's sympathetic attitude towards whatever of the True, the Beautiful, and the Good is contained in uncorrupted Buddhism, did not mislead him into committing the anachronism, for a Christian land and era, of reverting to Buddha as the supreme master, and thus subordinating the Light of the World to the Light of Asia.

Wagner's position in theological speculation may be compared to a Continental water-shed; for the more clearly we understand his position, so much the clearer and more far-reaching is our understanding of the course and destiny of the currents of thought which flow in various directions from that commanding height.

No study offers richer rewards to the cautious and clear-headed explorer than that of the various streams from which the children of men in all ages and climes have been accustomed to take their portion of the water of life which ever cometh down from above. Only we shall do well to avoid confounding the "ocean of commonplace," in which all religions alike find their lowest level, with the true point of unity discovered by following them upwards from the plane of ordinary human life to their sources along the way to the Throne above. For want of such precaution, Major-General Forlong, author of the monument of human research which he published under the title of "Rivers of Life," who went to India confident that he knew all, and that he was prepared to convert the heathen, made shipwreck of the faith, being, at the end of his far-reaching researches, unable, apparently, to see any thing in any religion beyond the external marks of all the degradations which all religions have suffered at the hands of the ignorant, the superstitious, and the debased; while, on the other hand, F. Max Müller, who may never have thought of converting anyone from one religion to another, has followed the currents of Hindu religion upward, until, reaching the plane of the highest ideas to which the Hindu ever attained, he has gained for us from those heights a new and open vision of the lofty superiority of Christianity, "towering o'er all the wrecks of time."

But apart from the interest and value attaching to the lines of thought opened up by an examination of Wagner's utterances upon the subject of Christianity, such an examination seems imperatively demanded by the prevalent ignorance, not only among cultivated people at large, but among music-lovers as well, and nowhere more pronounced than among admirers of Wagner's art, of the fact that he ever gave any thought to sacred subjects. Indeed, so certain were the editors of two influential newspapers that Wagner never had any religious opinions, that they had the temerity to review the present lecture without having heard a word of it, in supreme assurance that there was nothing to be said on the subject!

Thus, on the morning of the Sunday when this lecture was to be delivered, a Brooklyn journal placed before its readers the following editorial paragraph:

"A discourse on 'The Finding of Christ through Art; or, Richard Wagner as Theologian,' is announced for to-day at All Souls Episcopal Church in New York. Inasmuch as Wagner rejected Christianity and all other forms of religion, as he regarded utter annihilation or unconsciousness as the ideal destiny of man, and as he avowed a purpose to teach the philosophy of pessimism by his music, it would seem as if Dr. Heber Newton's pulpit guest had undertaken a somewhat difficult task."

While, at the distance of four hundred miles from New York, viz., in the city of Buffalo, a long newspaper editorial was printed, falsely purporting to report the lecture, the temper of which editorial will appear from the subjoined extracts:

"All Souls Church, New York, was filled with an audience which listened to the Gospel according to St. Richard. The particular Richard thus canonized was surnamed Wagner. . . . Like many another gospeller, he has begun to be misrepresented by his adherents since his death, even as he was falsified by his enemies while living. . . . Mr. Parsons asserted that the spirit of Christianity and of music alike was love, and hence drew the conclusion that their essential spirit was the same. Thence he argued that music, dispelling external things, brought the soul of man into direct and powerful communion with God. This is only one more rhapsody. Music has been mistaken for Christianity before now, and by much humbler persons than Mr. Parsons. To drop—or rise—from Wagner through prayer-meeting hymnology and the wild improvisation of the negro camp-meeting will illustrate the point where the lecturer missed the truth. Had he not missed it his lecture would never have been written. . . . The purposes of music and Christianity are not the same. . . . Mr. Parsons has attempted that inartistic labor which the . truest artists shun, of displaying art in places and in lights where it was never meant to be seen."

The reader who compares the lecture itself with these newspaper utterances will be prepared to follow Wagner where he writes (in his "Essay on Beethoven"):

"With the invention of newspapers, and since journalism has attained full bloom, the good spirit of the people has been forced to retire altogether from public life. For now only opinion rules, and indeed public opinion; it is to be had for money; . . . whoever takes a newspaper has procured not only the waste paper, but also its opinions; he no longer needs to think or to reflect; what he is to believe of God and the world is already thought out for him in black and white."

Touching the statement made by the reporter of a leading New York daily newspaper, that the lecturer said that, "From Wagner's thirtieth year on he studied Christianity until he became a sincere Christian," the present writer can only say that he does not know at what point in the lecture that remarkable affirmation was made! Without presuming to determine for others precisely what constitutes a "sincere Christian," he deems it exceedingly improbable that Wagner ever did become a Christian in any popular acceptation of the term. But that Wagner *found* the Christ, the Son of the Living God, of that the writer is convinced by the simple fact, among other things, that to his personal knowledge, the reading of this lecture at All Souls Church was the means of bringing into the sacred edifice certain intelligent persons, unaccustomed to church going, and in the habit of regarding Christianity as a mixture of delusion and conventionality, who subsequently confessed that Wagner's earnest words had illuminated their minds and caused their hearts to burn within them with a new sense of the meaning of Christianity as a great fact and factor, not only in civilization, past, present, and future, but also in personal life!

Over against all such *ex parte* newspaper statements, we may pause to place the conclusions to which the results of the present work will be found to point.

In the evolution of each individual human body, it passes through various phases in succession of definite resemblance to familar animal forms, and the body retains vestiges of some of those forms of existence through life; yet for all that, a man is not an animal, nor can an animal ever be a man. Something suggestive of this appears when we study the development of Wagner's religious thought. In his earlier years the nature of his studies and the natural revolt of conscious genius against prevalent abuses in political, artistic, and religious affairs brought him into contact at many points with the spirit of scepticism; yet Wagner was not a sceptic, nor can a sceptic ever be a Wagner.

To be sure, he, like many another great spirit, first saw only as through a glass, darkly; his soul had to

> " Draw from out the vast
> And strike his being into bounds,
> And—moved through life of lower phase—
> Result in man, be born and think."

But then, not having been destroyed by error, but like an Augustine of old, made wise by experience, he is gradually revealed to us as

> " No longer half-akin to brute ;
> For all he thought, and loved, and did,
> And hoped and suffered, was but seed
> Of what at last was flower and fruit
> For God, who ever lives and loves,
> One God, one law, one element,
> And one far-off divine event,
> To which the whole creation moves."
>
> *(In Memoriam.)*

For the Christian it must ever be a satisfaction to know that the thoughts we are about to follow from the writings of the grandest musical and dramatic genius who has appeared in modern times, are not early opinions accepted at the hands of teachers in youth, and subsequently disowned, but are the last utterances, at the ripe age of sixty-five years and upwards, of a mind of dauntless self-reliance, independence, and daring,—the deliberately expressed views of a man who detested conventionality and policy and showed the courage of his opinions at all times, regardless of consequences, and who withal was learned in and a master of the metaphysical science "which, certain professing, concerning their faith do swerve."

The Scriptural quotations which occur in these pages are mostly from " Young's Bible Translation," which, except in following convention in translating the titles of Deity in the Old Testament, aims at reproducing the Holy Oracles in English literally and in the exact idioms of the original.

GARDEN CITY, LONG ISLAND,
Lent, 1890.

PARSIFAL.

THE FINDING OF CHRIST THROUGH ART; OR, RICHARD WAGNER AS A THEOLOGIAN.*

In a sermon on "Inspiration," delivered in All Souls Church by the rector, Rev. R. Heber Newton, it was said : "Men of business, physicians, inventors, political economists, statesmen, novelists, dramatists, painters, musicians,—all may feel 'the inbreathing of the Divine Spirit, all may be most truly inspired.' Every knowledge and every power forms a step in the world's great altar stairs that 'slope through darkness up to God.' God claims all the varied fields of His own Creation as the spheres for His Spirit's action. All lines of true human thought focus in Religion."

We propose to subject this teaching to an apparently severe test, by taking the case of Richard Wagner, and examining the religious views to which,

* "In Christian phraseology *theologos* meets us first as the name of the author of the Apocalypse, John the Divine, or the *Theologos*. This name, however, we are told, was given to him not simply because he was what we call a theologian, but because he maintained the divinity of the Logos. In the third and fourth centuries *theologos* is said to have meant usually one who defended that doctrine." (F. Max Müller, "Natural Religion," 1889.)

solely as an artist, he was led, and upon which his last and loftiest creation, Parsifal, is based.

This is the Christian Sunday, and we are assembled in a Christian church. It is, therefore, neither the time nor the place for a panegyric either on Wagner or upon Art. Neither must this Church, its Lecture Chapter, nor the present speaker stand committed, even by implication, to any peculiarities in the ideas about to be presented for your consideration.

We are simply to examine the religious views finally reached by an artist who, orphaned in earliest youth and never systematically educated, became in the course of his favorite studies, in the field of the classical drama, so thoroughly a pagan at first that as late as 1849, at the age of thirty-six years, he expressly exalted the beautiful Greek god, Apollo, above Christ, as the true ideal of humanity.

"The Christian," said he, "rejects both Nature and Self. He can make offerings to his God only on the altar of renunciation; deeds he dare not bring. . . . While Jesus teaches the Brotherhood of Man, Apollo puts upon that Brotherhood the seal of strength and beauty, and leads mankind from doubt of their own worth, to the highest consciousness of their Divine power." (Wagner, "Collected Writings," Vol. III., pp. 20, 50.)

As, subsequently, Wagner created a series of works which, in spite of their alleged difficulty of comprehension, at present rule over the opera-houses of his native land, besides drawing lovers of

art from all lands to the remote Bavarian city where
he celebrated his crowning triumphs, and where his
ashes are entombed, it concerns us to ask the source
of his power. Was it culture or religion? Paganism
or Christianity? Was it of man or of God? Is or
is not, great art still, as of old, the handmaid of
religion?

That there is an ethical tendency in Wagner's
works is clear.

But, since it is a common idea that the actual un-
reality of theatrical representations tends to destroy
all belief in the reality of any thing ideal, two questions are asked by many, viz.:

1. Was not Wagner everywhere dealing, at least
in his own opinion, with mere myths?

2. Is not the ethical tendency in Wagner's works
a mere artistic calculation of stage-effect?

As to the first of these questions, namely, that of
dealing with " mere myths," it should be remembered
that there are various ways of looking at myths.

Thus in the *Popular Science Monthly* for February
and March of the current year (1890), under the
title of "Chapters in Comparative Mythology," by an
American College Ex-President, the writer seems
to take for granted that all myths are at bottom both
empty and false; and accordingly in the blundering
attempts made from time to time through the ages
to restate and explain those astonishing stories, the
memory of which an overruling Providence has
ordained, it would seem, that men shall preserve in

some form or other and hand down to times of greater light, in which both the original events and their moral shall at last be understood,—in all of this the *Popular Science* writer in question sees chiefly something over which to raise a laugh!

To all such barren views of the nature and significance of myths, it suffices to apply the words: "By their fruits ye shall know them!"

On the other hand we have the fruitful view of myths entertained by such great minds as Schelling, Ruskin, Wagner, etc.

Says Schelling, rejecting the notion that in myths we see simply the flower of human folly: "How, if in mythology the ruins of a superior intelligence and even a perfect system were found, which would reach far beyond the horizon which the most ancient written records present to us?"

Says Ruskin: "We may take it for a first principle both in science and literature, that the feeblest myth is better than the strongest theory: myth recording a natural impression on the imaginations of great men and unpretending multitudes, the theory an unnatural exertion of the wits of little men and the half-wits of impertinent multitudes. The myths, like all thoughts worth having, came like sunshine, whether people would or not: theories, like thoughts not worth having, are little lucifer matches people strike for themselves" (to "lighten their darkness," Ruskin might have added).

That these natural impressions, or myths, were no

mere poetic toys or trifles in Wagner's estimation is abundantly shown by his saying that "Feeling is the beginning and the end of understanding, as the *myth is the beginning and the end of history,* and tone-language the beginning and the end of word-language; the intermediate between beginning and middle-point, as also between middle-point and end, being imagination."   (" Wagner," IV., p. 114.)

Touching the second question, viz. : that of Wagner's personal sincerity in the ethical tendency of his works, we may cite three remarks.

The first states his attitude towards religion :

" The only religious liberty we claim, is liberty to deal seriously and honestly with holy things." (Wagner, " Baireuth Leaves," 1878, p. 36.)

The second citation is a bit of counsel to young dramatic composers, disclosing his own personal methods :

" I never have been able to compose at all before something had occurred to me.   I would say to the young composer, never adopt a text before you have found in it an action carried on by persons in whom you take a lively interest.   Of these persons, regard with closest scrutiny the one who interests you most in the light of to-day.   If it wears a mask, away with it ; if it appears in theatrical costume, tear it off !   Place the figure in the twilight, so as to perceive only the glance of its eye, and now the shape itself will manifest a vitality which may perhaps startle you, but that is something you will have to put up with; and now its lips will move, and a spirit voice will say to you something real and thoroughly comprehensible, yet never before heard, as did once, say, the Marble Guest, and the page Cherubino, to Mozart. On hearing this, you will awaken as from a dream. Every thing will vanish from sight, but in the spiritual hearing the message will sound on. Something has occurred to you, and that is a musical motive." ("Wagner," 1879, p. 264.)

Our third citation throws light on the question of mere calculation of stage-effect, by disclosing Wagner's conscious attitude toward the amusement-seeking public:

"When I am alone by myself, and the musical fibres begin to tremble within me, when confused sounds shape themselves into harmonies, and from those harmonies arises the melody which, as Idea, reveals to me my whole being; when the heart in loud beatings adds its impetuous metre, and inspiration pours itself out in divine tears through the mortal eye, which now no longer sees,—then I often say to myself: 'What a great fool art thou, not to keep always by thyself and dwell there in these unique joys, instead of pressing out into that hideous crowd called the public! What can that public, even with its most brilliant receptions, give to thee, which will possess even the hundreth part of the value of that sacred refreshing which wells up within thyself?'" ("Wagner," I., p. 223.)

Before proceeding to exhibit the Christian theology to which Wagner was led by his labors in the field of musical drama, it is proper to say a word to those who, affected by the conduct popularly attributed to him, may be startled by the idea of considering him in the light of a Christian theologian. Suffice it to say, that certainly for years previous to the expression of the religious conclusions which we are about to consider, Wagner lived subject to the forms of German law, and under the formal sanction of the Protestant Church of Germany. That is all which we, as good citizens, are concerned to know. The rest is a matter between Richard Wagner and the Divine Redeemer, whom he learned to confess before his fellow-men in words and tones of glowing enthusiasm.

"Only in his deeds," says Wagner, "are the thoughts of a man convincingly revealed. Precisely in the perfect agreement between his thoughts and his deeds does his character consist." ("Wagner," IV., p. 43.)

We have already remarked the ethical quality of Wagner's artistic deeds, and we are now to follow the thoughts which resulted from his pursuing art up to the point of its vital union with Christianity.

At the very outset of our investigation the reader may find it hard to postpone the question : Did Wagner himself become a Christian ? To answer that question satisfactorily, perhaps we should first all have to agree as to what is essential to Christianity. Roman Catholic he was not, nor was he either Churchman, Presbyterian, or Unitarian. His lofty admiration for the genius of Luther, as a foremost representative of German spirit, in the courage of its convictions and its "irrepressible protest against all external burdens laid upon it" of a formalistic nature, is well known to all students of Wagner's writings; but, for all that, his plane of vision was such that he viewed neither life nor religion through Lutheran spectacles exclusively, but, instead, drew many a profound lesson from the lives and teaching of Roman Catholic saints.

Indeed, there are so many sorts of Christians now, that it seems just as impossible for all of us to be of one sort as for one of us to be of all sorts. *It would seem, however, that we may all of us either find, or fail to find, the Christ.* If we shall conclude that Wagner found the Christ, perhaps we may defer the question of his Christianity until we have settled among ourselves the question of our own.*

A *thinker* on Christianity, Wagner unquestionably became. If we further ask, what sort of thinker he became, and whether he, self-taught in theology, came to think as all think who ever think at all upon Christianity, the questions answer themselves. God is obviously not the author of confusion, with its necessary consequence—endless sameness, but, instead, of unity in boundless diversity. Hence, while all Chris-

---

* For testing the quality of one's own religious life, a simple criterion is afforded by F. Max Müller's concentrated definition of Religion as "*a perception of the infinite under such manifestations as are able to influence the moral character of men.*"

tians may be united in charity, the only ones who can think just alike are those who never think at all, beyond the point of thinking it best to let others do their thinking for them.

Wagner thought for himself. Hence, what he brought to light is in the native ore, and full of elements characteristic of his own personality. To the degree, however, that this ore contains real gold, its intrinsic value will be obvious, even in the absence of the form and impress of products of an authorized theological mint.

A convenient point of departure for our investigation is offered by Wagner's view of the attitude of physical science toward the least animal and most truly human side of human nature, viz., the spiritual side. Says Wagner, with keen irony:

"Since, with the advance of physical science, all the mysteries of being must necessarily be exposed as merely imaginary mysteries, nothing will be left but knowledge, and even then intuitive knowledge will have to be excluded, since it might lead to metaphysical assumptions from which abstract scientific knowledge must be kept free, *until logic, guided by chemistry* (!) has become clear concerning intuitive knowledge! To the Goliath of modern science, art daily becomes more and more of a mere rudiment of a former cognitive stage of human life, a sort of tail-bone surviving in us from an actual prehensile tail of earlier times. Hence this Goliath only indulges in intercourse with art so far as is necessary

for the maintenance of academies, colleges, etc., honestly doing his best, meanwhile, to prevent any thing
like true artistic productivity from arising, *because
that might all too easily induce a relapse into the
'inspiration swindle' of surmounted periods of culture!*"   ("Wagner," 1878, p. 218.)

But, does some one exclaim : Is not modern science
the champion of progress? Let us hear Wagner again :

"Those who float with the stream may fancy they
belong to the party of continual progress. It is, at
all events, easy to let themselves be borne along by
the current, and they do not notice that their destiny
is to be swallowed up in the ocean of the commonplace. To swim against the stream must seem ridicu-
lous to all who are not irresistibly impelled to make
the enormous effort which is required to do it. But
we really cannot prevent being swept away by the
current save by swimming against it toward the true
source of life. Often it will seem impossible to
avoid succumbing; but just as often we shall emerge
from the waves and find ourselves rescued at the
moment of deepest exhaustion—and lo! the aston-
ished waves will hear a voice, and for a moment
stand still, as when a great spirit unexpectedly speaks
to the world! Then the bold swimmer will again
strike out, not life, but the true source of life
being his quest! Who that has once reached that
source could ever find pleasure in again plunging
into that current? From blissful heights he looks
down upon the distant ocean with its mutually-

destroying monsters. Can we blame him for renouncing forever all that there destroys itself ? " (" Wagner," 1878, p. 285.)

Wagner was a student of the dramatic art of the Greeks from boyhood on. It was, therefore, but natural that he should finally approach Christianity by the same path as did the ancient Greeks, who, occupying by virtue of the cultivation of mythology a plane of thought superior to any merely materialistic, physical view of life, developed a metaphysic which rendered the doctrine of Incarnation at once rational and philosophical. Says Wagner :

" Of the Greek belief in gods it may be said that, conformably to their artistic endowments, that belief was always combined with anthropomorphism, or the manifestation of the Divine in human form. Their gods were well-defined shapes of the most distinct individuality, and the names of those gods designated the notion of a species precisely as names of colored objects designated the different colors themselves, for which the Greeks employed no abstract names, such as ours. Gods they were called only to designate their nature as Divine. The Divine Himself, however, the Greeks called simply God. It never occurred to them to think of God as limited to personality. Hence they never gave Him an artistic shape, like the gods with names. God Himself was left to the philosophers to define, and proved a conception which the Hellenic mind sought in vain distinctly to establish,* until, by a band of wonderfully inspired poor people, the incredible tidings were proclaimed that the Son of God had offered himself upon the Cross as a sacrifice for the redemption of the world from the bonds of deceit and sin. With this, God Himself assumed shape in the most anthropomorphic manner, viz., the highest conception of sympathetic love embodied in a human form stretched in agonizing sufferings upon the Cross. In this picture, and its effect upon the soul, lies the entire magic by which the Church first conquered the Græco-Roman world." ("Wagner," 1880, p. 272.)

The full measure of Wagner's worship of Christ we cannot learn without listening to his views concerning the reason why the Redeemer is not yet found "chief among ten thousand and altogether lovely" by mankind in general, and by many of the choicest minds of all ages in particular. In following him on this point, we must continually bear in mind that to Wagner, a self-taught theologian, the names of God and Jehovah were not synonymous

---

* "And Paul, having stood in the midst of the Areopagus, said, Men, Athenians, in all things I perceive you as over-religious ; for passing through and contemplating your objects of worship, I found also an erection on which had been inscribed ' To God—unknown ': whom, therefore—not knowing,—ye do worship, this one I announce to you . . . He giving to all life, and breath, and all things : He made also of one blood every nation of men, to dwell upon all the face of the earth—having ordained times before appointed, and the bounds of their dwellings—to seek the Lord, if perhaps they did feel after Him and find,—though, indeed, he is not far off from each one of us, for in Him we live and move, and are : as also certain of your poets have said : For of Him we also are offspring." (Acts, xvii., 22–23, 25–28.)

in meaning. His train of thought here compels us to distinguish between the true Jehovah and a false Jehovah, who was the reflection of the personal character of His worshippers.

Says a modern writer : " Man-created Gods are wonderful beings. They possess all the virtues and vices of those who make them, and they in return cause those who create them to be vicious or virtuous, foolish or wise, as the case may be. From the time of the Babylonian captivity, a curse seems to have been attached to the Jewish nation. They excel other nations in such virtues as grow from a state of separateness and isolation ; they cling closely to each other; they assist each other in need ; they love their families, and they are heroes in the defence of what they may legally claim as their own. Yet they have been persecuted in almost every country, and have met with hatred wherever they went.

" If we attempt to trace to its origin the curse which seems to have rested upon them, we may find it in the fact, that instead of worshipping the true Jehovah, who rejoices within the hearts of men when they kill their animal passions and sacrifice to Him their erroneous opinions; they created, after the pattern of the gods of other peoples, a cruel, bloodthirsty God, whom they called Jehovah, and the God whom they created reflected upon them his own attributes, and became the instrument of their punishment. In creating a separate God of their own, isolated from the God of Humanity, who is no respecter of persons, but has in every nation those who fear Him they became themselves isolated. The God who was the outcome of their own selfishness became the instrument of their torture.

"In vain arose to the clouds the odor of burning bullocks and sheep from the altars of their temples. By the mouth of the prophet Jeremiah, the true Jehovah of Hosts and God of Israel declared unto them explicitly: 'I did not speak with your fathers, Nor did I command them in the day of my bringing them out of the land of Egypt, Concerning the matters of burnt-offerings and sacrifice, But this thing I commanded them, saying, Hearken to my voice, and I will be unto you for God and ye shall be my people and shall walk in the way I command you, and it shall be well with you.' But to the Jehovah of Jeremiah, Israel did not hearken; and the false Jehovah, the mental image which they endowed with their own character, had no power to help his worshippers. The Unlimited, Eternal, and Infinite God disappeared from their view, and they endowed the false Jehovah with all the good and evil qualities which characterized their own selves. Thus the eternal Reality, the Truth, was deposed from His throne, the prophets were stoned, and priestcraft, with its opiates and illusions, assumed the sceptre. Thus the worshippers of the false Jehovah forfeited their own manhood. The interests of the Jewish Church became paramount to the pursuit of wisdom; external ceremonies and material sacrifices took the place of spiritual aspirations and heart-offerings."

All of this Wagner seems to have seen; and he further saw how far the Hebrews remained from realizing the idea of an immanent God, such as Theism teaches, and that they rather conceived of God deistically, taking so literally the command, " Thou hast no other gods before me ! " that they recognized the existence of "other gods" by repeatedly and flagrantly disobeying the injunction, and worshipping them. It is, therefore, only unusual, but by no means inexplicable, that Wagner should have failed to recognize in Jehovah of the Jews the God and Father of our Lord and Saviour Jesus Christ; for did not the Lord Himself say: " Nor doth any know the Father, except the Son, and he to whom the Son may wish to reveal Him "? Accordingly, we shall represent Wagner's exact meaning more precisely by translating, "The Tribal Deity of the Jews," or the "God of Deism," wherever Wagner refers to "Jehovah." It will be observed that in Wagner's opinion, materialistic physical science is destructive of Deism only, while Christian Theism is wholly beyond its reach. Wagner writes:

" That which necessarily led to the downfall of the Church and finally to the continually more pronounced Atheism of our time, was the idea inspired by the mania for conquest, of deriving this Divinity on the Cross from the Tribal Deity of the Jews, with the preaching of whom, as an angry and vindictive

God, it seemed to the priests possible to accomplish
more than with the preaching of the self-offer-
ing, all-loving Saviour of the poor." ("Wagner,"
1880, p. 272.) "That the God of our Saviour should
be declared to us as identical with the Tribal Deity
of Israel is one of the most frightful confusions in
the history of the world. It has in all ages revenged
itself, and to-day still revenges itself in the continually more and more outspoken Atheism of the
coarsest as well as the finest minds. Science is
making the god of Deism continually more and more
impossible. Meanwhile, the God revealed by Jesus
has from the birth of the Church been progressively
reduced by theologians from the most sublime obvi-
ousness, to a continually more and more unintelligible problem." ("Wagner," 1878, p. 219.)

"The Gospels have now been so often and so
exactly examined critically, and their origin and the
facts concerning their compilation brought out with
such unmistakable correctness, that in the midst of
all that excites contradiction as ungenuine and extra-
neous, the sublime form of the Redeemer and His
work, must, it seem to us, have become distinctly
apparent to the critics themselves. But the God
revealed to us by Jesus, *the God which none of the
gods, sages, or heroes of the world ever knew*, but
who now, in the very midst of the Pharisees, Scribes,
and Priests, was revealed to poor Galilean fishermen
and shepherds with such power and simplicity, that
whoever once discerned Him, immediately looked

upon the world with all its possessions, as worthless
and null,—this God, *who never can be revealed
again, because then and for the first time, He was
revealed to mankind,* this God the critics forever
view with mistrust, because they deem themselves
compelled to identify Him with the Tribal Deity
of the Jews and Deistic Creator of the world."
("Wagner," 1878, pp. 219–220.)

"This confusion of thought is so great, that it is
really astonishing to see how the most important
minds of all times, since the appearance of the Bible,
have been cramped by it and betrayed into weakness
of judgment. Think of Goethe, who deemed Christ
problematical, but held the God of Deism to be
a demonstrated fact ! In so concluding, Goethe reserved, to be sure, the liberty to find that God in his
own way in Nature. This of course always results
in all sorts of physical experiments in the field of
natural science, the continual prosecution of which
experiments has again led the ruling human intellect
of the day to the conclusion that there is no God at
all, but only Force and Matter." ("Wagner," 1880,
p. 336.)

"The God of Deism was condemned by art. The
Deity in the burning bush, nay, even the white-
bearded venerable old man looking down out of a
cloud, with a blessing on his Son, did not, even when
represented by the most masterly artistic hand, say
much to the faithful soul: but the suffering God
upon the Cross, the 'Head bowed down with sor-

rows,' even in the crudest representation, still fills us as in all ages, with enthusiastic emotion." (" Wagner," 1880, p. 273.)

"The men of physical science feel very wise over the fact that Copernicus with his planetary system has taken away from God his heavenly home. We do not find, however, that the Church has felt materially perplexed by this discovery. For her and all the faithful, God still dwells in heaven, or as Schiller sings, ' Above the starry zone.' But the God within the human breast, of whom our greatest mystics have always been so certainly and luminously conscious over and above all consciousness of being, this God who needs no scientifically demonstrable heavenly habitation, has made trouble for the priests. To us Germans that God had become profoundly known. Still our professors have done much to spoil Him. They are now cutting up dogs to demonstrate Him to us in the spinal cord ! . . ." ("Wagner," 1880, p. 4.)

" Nevertheless, our own God, still evokes much within us, and as [in the confusion wrought by materialistic physical science] He was about to vanish from our sight, He left us for an eternal memorial of Himself our music, which is the living God in our bosoms. Hence we preserve our music and ward off from it all sacrilegious hands ; for if we harken to frivolous or insincere music we extinguish the last light God has left burning within us to lead the way to find Him anew !" (" Wagner," 1880, p. 274.)

We are not to understand Wagner to mean that hearing good music will reform a man's character and renew a right spirit within him. Lectures on æsthetics may help one to appreciate and honor art, but no one knew better than Wagner that to become an artist one must be not only a hearer, but also a doer of the word, developing one's individual powers by a diligent use of suitable means. In like manner, although in a materialistic age, holy music, as a witness of the indwelling spirit, may lead the way to find God anew, religious perceptions alone will not ensure personal attainments in religion : that only a diligent use of suitable religious and devotional means can do. The Church would have an easy task before her in laboring for the regeneration of mankind if sinners could be turned into saints simply by hearing good sermons and good music.

Concerning the historic origin of music and what the divine art may say to the feeling heart, we cite the following sayings of Wagner's :

" **The Christian Church** bequeathed to the world as her noblest treasure, music, the all-plaintive, all-saying, sounding soul of the Christian Religion. Flying abroad from within her temple walls, holy music goes forth breathing new life into every part of Nature." (" Wagner," 1880, p. 298 :) " To-day art thou with me in Paradise." Who does not hear the Redeemer's words call to him as he listens to Beethoven's Pastoral symphony? The effect upon the listener is precisely that of emancipation from

all guilt, just as the after effect with which we return
to everyday life is the feeling of a Paradise lost. So
does music preach repentance and amendment of life
in the profoundest sense of a divine revelation. As
Christianity arose under the Roman universal civilization, so music bursts forth from the chaos of a
heartless, materialistic modern civilization. The
spirit of both Christianity and music is Love; and
both affirm, 'Our kingdom is not of this world.'
We are from within, you from without; we are the
offspring of the essential nature of things, you of the
semblance of things. Thus music excites within us,
as soon as we are filled with it, the highest ecstasy of
the consciousness of illimitability. As soon as the
first measures only of one of Beethoven's divine
symphonies are heard, the entire phenomenal world,
which impenetrably hems us in on every side, suddenly vanishes into nothingness; music extinguishes
it as sunshine does lamplight. In music's enig-
matically entwined lines and wonderfully intricate
characters stand written the eternal symbols of
a new and different world." (Wagner's "Beethoven.")

"Above all thinkableness by means of concepts of
Reason, the musical seer, 'speaking the highest wisdom in a language which Reason does not comprehend,' reveals to us the inexpressible truth; while
we listen we have a presentiment; nay, we feel and
see that this seemingly substantial world of the
Will is only a fleeting show in the presence of the

one truth, 'I know that my Redeemer liveth.'"
("Wagner," 1880, p. 298.)

Wagner seems to have found reason for making a
vigorous protest against intellectual stagnation in the
preaching of Christianity in the pulpits of Germany.
He writes :

"What a dismal, nay, unworthy, position our
entire theology now occupies since our ecclesiastical
teachers and popular preachers have ceased to con-
tribute to it much of any thing besides material
for a disingenuous explanation of our most precious
Gospels. For what purpose is the preacher in
the chancel save to make compromises between
things involving the deepest contradictions, the sub-
tleties of which necessarily undermine faith itself, so
that finally we are forced to ask : Who, then, still
knows Jesus? The historical critics, think you?
Why, they stand in the midst of Judaism ('Wagner,'
1878, p. 220), declaring that with a sinless Jesus
they do not know what to do ('Wagner,' 1880, p.
285) ; and they marvel to themselves precisely as does
every Hebrew, that early Sunday mornings the bells
still ring for a Jew crucified two thousand years
ago !" ("Wagner," 1878, p. 219.)

In connection with the foregoing paragraphs we
may place the following observations as of importance to all who would seek to explain the appearance of prophets, teachers, etc., substantially in
accordance with the doctrine of Evolution as it is
applied to the physical world. Says Wagner:

" The scientifico-historic school assumes to demonstrate that every eminent individual must needs be
the product of the spirit of the race to which he
belongs and of his environment in Time and Space.
The correctness of the assumption does not seem
rationally deniable. It only remains for the critics
to explain why the greater the individual, so much
the greater the contradiction with his time in which
he finds himself involved." (" Wagner," 1878, p. 277.)
" To cite the sublimest of examples : neither the con-
temporary world nor his own race deported themselves towards Christ as if they had brought Him
forth and rejoiced to recognize in Him a typical
product of their own." (" Wagner," 1878, p.
287.)

With Wagner, human wisdom does not count for
every thing.

" The Founder of the Christian Religion was not
wise : He was Divine. To believe in Him is to
imitate Him, and to seek union with Him."
(" Wagner," 1880, pp. 270–271.)

" In consequence of His atoning death, every thing
which lives and breathes may know itself redeemed
as soon as the Redeemer is accepted as example and
pattern for life." (" Wagner," 1879, p. 365.) " Among
the poorest and most isolated people the Saviour
appeared showing the way of redemption, not by
doctrines but by His own example." (" Wagner,"
1880, p. 283). " So the true saint knows, that neither
by theorizing, disputation, nor controversy, can he

communicate to the world his inner, deeply blissful intuitions in such a way as to convince the world of their genuineness. He can do it only by example, by deeds of self-renunciation and self-sacrifice, and by the manifestation of unalterable gentleness, and of a sublime, serene seriousness diffused throughout his labors. There is therefore a profound and true meaning in the idea that only through their beloved saints can the people turn to God. The saint, the martyr, the exemplar, are the true mediums of healing. In them the people may recognize in the only way comprehensible to them what must be the contents of the religious perceptions in which they can participate only by faith, instead of by direct personal knowledge." (" Wagner," VIII., p. 33.)

" We must assume," continues he, "that the Idea, or rather, the immediate perception of the religious seer, so indescribably beneficent in its effect, yet only to be comprehended in the category of illusion, remains both as to its form and content, wholly foreign and incomprehensible to the common mind. Hence, all that can be announced by, or about, those ideas or perceptions, to the profane, to the masses, must necessarily be nothing else than a sort of allegory, as it were a translation of things inexpressible, never seen, and only intelligible through direct intuition, into the language of ordinary life and forms of knowledge intrinsically erroneous yet alone possible to them." (" Wagner," VIII., p. 29.)

" The only element of Revelation which the world

at large can grasp is Dogma. In this sacred allegory it is sought to convey to worldly minds the mysteries of Divine revelation. This sacred allegory is related to the immediate vision of the seer, only as the account of a dream while awake, is related to the actual dream of the night. (VIII., p. 30.) The conflict running through the centuries, touching the correctness and rationality of Dogma, affords us the painfully repulsive instruction of the history of the illness of a maniac. Two modes of perception and knowledge, absolutely incongruous and in their nature entirely different, are entangled in this controversy, without its being perceived that they are fundamentally different. In this conflict, the truly religious defenders of Dogma are right, as far as they proceed on principle from a consciousness that their mode of knowledge is different from all mere worldly knowledge; while the terrible wrong into which they have suffered themselves to be driven, lies in the fact, that as they could do nothing with everyday human reason, they have allowed themselves to be carried away by passionate zeal into the most inhuman abuse of power, and so have degenerated into a state the most completely opposite to that of holiness. On the other hand, we are indebted for the comfortless, materialistic, empty, and wholly Godless condition of the modern industrial world, to the opposite zeal of a common practical reason, which seeks to explain Dogma in accordance with the causal laws of everyday life, and rejects all which resists such explanation as senseless brain cobwebs!" (" Wagner," VIII., pp. 31, 32.)

Turning now from the Divinity of Christ and the Indispensability of Religious Dogma or Doctrine, let us consider what Wagner has to say of the Christian virtues. He writes:

" The Christian commandments are quite clearly exhibited in the so-called Theological Virtues. Yet these are presented to us in an order which does not seem to us quite right for the purpose of an introduction to Christianity; for we would like to see Faith, Hope, and Love transposed to Love, Faith, and Hope. The degree of merit involved in acquiring these virtues we soon perceive when we reflect what an almost superfluous demand is made upon the natural man by the command to 'Love,' in the sublime sense of Christianity. What is the disease from which our entire civilization suffers, but want of love? As the youthful soul learns with ever-increasing distinctness to know the modern world, he may indeed ask, how can he love it? since mistrust and precaution are everywhere commended to him for self-protection in his intercourse with the world. There certainly is but one way open before him, viz., that of recognizing that the essential cause of the unloveliness in the world lies in the sufferings which are in the world. Pity awakened by those sufferings implies a conscious renunciation of their cause, namely, the cravings of our passions,—in order that we may do our part

towards ameliorating and warding off the sufferings
of others.   But how is the natural man to attain to
such perceptions, seeing that the most inexplicable
thing of all is our fellow-man ?   Truly, the natural
man cannot be led to the duty of self-sacrifice by
commandment.   He can only be brought to the
fulfilment of that duty by a right understanding
of the origin of all living beings.   Here, to the best
of our knowledge, a wise use of Schopenhauer's
philosophy is the surest, nay, almost the sole way to
attain to a rational understanding of the problem,
the result of that philosophy alone, to the shame of
all other systems be it said, being the recognition of
a moral significance to the world, such as (the crown
of all knowledge !) is practicably deducible from
Schopenhauer's Ethics." ("Wagner," 1880, p. 338.)
"Only love rooted in sympathy, and expressed in
action to the point of a complete destruction of
self-will, is Christian Love."   ("Wagner," 1880, p.
339.)   "In it Faith and Hope are of themselves
included ; Faith as the infallibly sure consciousness,
confirmed by the Divinest Prototype, of the moral
significance of the world ; and Hope as the blissful
assurance of the impossibility of any deception in
the consciousness of Faith."   ("Wagner," 1880, p.
338.)

   Closely connected in idea with what has been
cited from Wagner concerning human unloveliness
as the expression of human suffering, are the following observations :

" When at last we necessarily recognize in the people the artists of the future, the intelligent artistic egotist of the present day breaks out in contemptuous astonishment. He views the people only in the shape in which they now appear before his culture-bespectacled eyes. From his sublime standpoint he believes that his own antithesis, the raw common man, alone constitutes the people. Hence in glancing at them he is only aware of the fumes of beer and bitters in his nose. He seizes his perfumed handkerchief, and with civilized indignation exclaims : ' What ! the mob will eventually replace us in artistic productivity ! That mob which does not even understand our artistic wares ! From the nauseous tavern and the steaming dung-hill, the types of beauty shall arise ! ' "

" Quite right ! " (rejoins Wagner) " not from the dirty substratum of your modern culture, not from the repulsive soil beneath your modern fine education, not from the conditions which your modern civilization deems the sole conceivable basis of human existence, will the art-work of the future arise. Reflect, however, that this mob is in no wise a normal product of real human nature, but, instead, the artificial product of your unnatural culture ; that all the crimes and horrors which you find so repulsive in this mob, are only desperate incidents of the war which real human-nature is waging against its cruel oppressor—modern civilization ; and that the terrifying feature in their grimaces is in no

wise the true mien of nature, but instead, the direct
reflex of the grimaces of our State and Criminal
culture."

The scientific doctrine of the Transformation and
Equivalence of Force, Wagner applies to the problem in hand, as follows :

" As long as you intelligent egotists of fine culture
bloom in an artificial atmosphere, so long there must
necessarily be the human material from whose vital
forces your sweet perfume of life is distilled; and
that material from which for your benefit its natural
and agreeable vital fragrance is abstracted, necessarily
becomes the ill-smelling refuse of human life whose
presence rightly disgusts you, but from which you
are distinguishable mainly by the perfume which
you have pressed out of their natural cheerfulness.
As long as a large part of the entire people wastes
costly vital power in useless occupations, so long
must an equally large, if not a larger, part be over-
taxed with necessary labor in order to replace by its
own toil the work wasted or evaded by others. But
this is not all; for when among the inordinately
burdened workingmen the useful, that which serves
utility alone, becomes the sole end of activity, the
soul of life itself, the revolting spectacle must follow
of absolute egotism everywhere making the laws of
life, while with hateful grimaces it grins back to law-
makers from the countenances of town and country
mobs ! Neither the pampered few nor the vulgar
mob do we mean when we speak of the people.

"The Jesuits give to pupils on entering their schools, as their first and foremost concern, the occupation of representing to themselves, devoutly, and with the exertion of all their powers of soul, assisted by the most ingenious and effective aids, the idea of eternal damnation. On the other hand, a Parisian workingman whom, for breaking his word, I once threatened with hell, replied : ' Oh, sir, hell is on this earth ! ' Our great Schopenhauer was of the same opinion, and found in Dante's ' Inferno ' the world in which we live strikingly portrayed. In truth, the religious teachers of our youth would proceed much more to the purpose if they began by explaining this world and our life distinctly and with Christian sympathy to young hearts, instead of trying to awaken in them the fear of a future hell as the source of all virtues." ("Wagner," 1879, p. 124.)

In Paris, in 1836 (as Wagner once confessed to Liszt), thievish longings "often possessed him " on watching the dawn of the hot days that were to "shine" on his "empty stomach." To what Wagner has to say further concerning the people in their unloveliness caused by suffering, a suitable introduction is afforded by the Saviour's words to the egotists and lovers of themselves : " I did hunger, and ye gave me not to eat; I did thirst, and ye gave me not to drink; a stranger I was, and ye did not receive me; naked, and ye put not around me; infirm and in prison, and ye did not look after me. Then shall they answer, saying, Lord, when did we see thee hungering, or thirsting, or a stranger, or naked, or infirm, or in prison, and we did not minister to thee? Then shall he answer them, saying, Verily I say to you, inasmuch as ye did it not to one of these, the least, ye did it not to me." Says Wagner:

"Could our scientific investigator, regaining sincerity from the contemplation of animals, turn his gaze to the multitudes of his really suffering fellow-men, who—born in naked want, and from earliest childhood driven to health-destroying and excessive toil, while prematurely enfeebled by bad food and heartless treatment of all sorts,—look up questioningly to him in mute submission, perhaps our man of science would then say to himself: 'This being is also human, like myself.' That would indeed be a success. If then we cannot emulate the sympathizing animal which voluntarily starves with its master, let us at all events try to surpass the animal by helping the poor to their necessary food, as might easily be done if we could place them on the same diet with the rich by contriving to hand over to them the excess of food which at present makes the rich sick! But we cultivate needless sciences only. Upon prolonging to a certain distant day the life of a dying Hungarian magnate depended the fate of enormous claims to inheritance. The interested parties offered rich rewards to the doctors to prolong the man's life to that day. Here was a chance for science! God only knows how much bleeding and poisoning was done. They triumphed! The

inheritance was ours ! Science was brilliantly remu-
nerated. It must not be assumed that so much
science ought to be employed for the relief of our
poor workingmen ! " * ("Wagner," 1879, p. 309.)

In following Wagner further in his utterances
upon economic questions, it is interesting to note
that in the ancient order of things upon which he
dwells with evident approbation, neither communism
nor unqualified rights of private property obtained.
The right of possession was regulated by the needs,
not the luxurious cravings, of the individual. Among
conquering races, all excess of spoils was awarded to
those who rendered distinguished services to the
community.

Of the *rôle* played in history by possessions,
Wagner writes :

"From possessions which have become private
property, and which now, strangely enough, are
regarded as the very foundation of good order,
spring all the crimes, both of myth and of history."
("Wagner," IV., p. 82.)

"Thus in the Nibelung Myth we recognize the
view, drawn with uncommon distinctness, of all
those races by which that myth was invented,
developed, and matured, concerning the nature of

* If the Emperor William III., who is an open patron of Wagner's art
at Baireuth, shall succeed in evolving a method whereby to put an end to
the cruelties of industrial slavery, and secure to real workingmen a due
amount of work with reasonable hours, together with an amount of com-
pensation which will both encourage and enable them to live, though
humbly, yet like men, the homage of a world will attest anew how much
greater are the victories of peace than those of war.

possessions and private property. While in the most
ancient, religious view, the treasure-hoard represents
the splendors of earth revealed by sunlight, we find
it later on, in poetic form, as the might-giving spoils
of the hero, which, as the reward for the most daring
and astonishing deeds, he has won by overcoming a
cruel foe. This hoard, this might-giving possession,
is thenceforth craved by the descendants of the
divine hero; but it is in the highest degree characteristic, that the possessions are never acquired by
them in indolence, but instead only by deeds similar
to those of the first winner. These views, in accordance with which man was originally ennobled, and
conceived to be an initial point of all power, corre-
spond entirely with the mode in which anciently
possessions were disposed of in real life. While, in
the remotest antiquity, the natural and simple principle obtained of regulating the measure of the right
of possession or of enjoyment in accordance with
the needs, not the luxurious cravings of the individual, it was no less natural that among conquering races, wherever there was an excess of
spoils, the might and daring of the most famous war-
rior should be deemed to entitle him to a richer and
more luxurious share. In the historic application of
the feudal system we still see, as long as it lasted in
its original purity, the heroic-man principle distinctly
expressed: the bestowal of favors was solely upon
the one man who could lay claim to them by reason
of some great deed done, some important service

rendered. From the instant that fiefs became subject to inheritance, men, as regards personal valor and deeds, lost in worth, this passing over to their possessions instead. Their possessions, acquired by inheritance, not their virtues as individuals, gave to their descendants their importance; and the consequently steadily deeper depreciation of the man over against the steadily higher appreciation of his possessions, were finally embodied in the most inhuman of arrangements, such as the right of primogeniture. It is from this strangely reversed order of things that the later nobility have imbibed all their arrogance and pride, without considering that just because their worth is derived from petrified family possessions, they have openly denied and rejected real human nobility. But what a cruelly inhuman form the right of private property now assumes in our haggling world of machine-factories, in which, to speak precisely, workingmen are men only to the extent which the demands of capital will permit! ('Wagner,' I., p. 196.) And now, according to the conscience of the State, property has greater sanctity than religion. For injury to the cause of religion there is toleration; but for injury to property-rights only the most merciless severity. ('Wagner,' 1881, p. 39.) Our God is gold; and money-getting is our religion." ("Wagner," III., p. 34.)

And now we have, in Wagner's words, "the terribly amazing spectacle of seeing a philosophy like Schopenhauer's, which is based on a perfect ethics, felt to be 'hopeless,' whence it follows that we would like to be hopeful without a knowledge of true morality." (" Wagner," 1880, p. 336.)

After Wagner's endorsement of Schopenhauer's Ethics, it is interesting to hear what Schopenhauer has to say touching the matter of rights between man and man.

" A bad man," says Schopenhauer, " is a man who has so high a degree of egotism that he seeks his own well-being alone, while completely indifferent to the interests of others, whose existence is to him altogether foreign and divided from his own by a wide gulf, and who are regarded by him as mere masks with no reality behind them." (" World as Will and Idea," Book IV., p. 468.) Thus the bad man, " the egotist, feels himself surrounded by strange and hostile individuals, and all his hope is centred in his own good. The good man, on the contrary, lives in a world of friendly individuals, the well-being of any of whom he regards as his own." (" World as Will and Idea," Book IV., p. 483.) " The essential char-acter of his conduct is that he makes less distinction than is usually made between himself and others." (" World as Will and Idea," Book IV., p. 480.) Thus, while egotism is unsympathetic, all love is sympathy. " The teaching of this kind which lies nearest to hand is Christianity, the ethics of which lead not only to the highest degree of human love, but also to renunciation, perfect indifference to worldly things, dying to our own will and being born into God." ("World as Will and Idea," Book IV., p. 499.)

The foregoing passage is worthy of the great Schopenhauer, who said : "There is nothing in which one has to distinguish the kernel so carefully from the shell as in Christianity. Just because I prize this kernel highly, I sometimes treat the shell with little ceremony ; it is, however, thicker than is generally supposed." ("World as Will and Idea," Vol. III., p. 447.) " Christianity belongs to the ancient, true, and sublime faith of mankind, which is opposed to the false, shallow, and injurious optimism which exhibits itself in Greek paganism, Judaism, and Islamism." ("World as Will and Idea," Vol. III., p. 446.)

Touching egotism in religion, Wagner, whose "artistic nature" (we quote his words) "and the sufferings it had had to undergo, had opened his eyes to see into the deepest depth of things in such a manner that death alone could ever close them again," * writes as follows :

* The last letter written by Wagner is dated January 31, 1883, thirteen days before his death. It is addressed to Von Stein, who had written a work, " Heroes and the World," in a series of dramatic scenes. Wagner approved this setting of history in a dramatic frame, and one sentence of his letter is : " No step in advance is more pregnant with success than that from reflecting like a philosopher to seeing like a dramatist. To see, to see, to really see ; here is where they all fail ! ' Have you eyes?' is a question that may be forever addressed to this eternally chattering and listening world, in which gaping takes the place of seeing. Whoever has really seen knows how he stands with it.

" One hour of real, true seeing taught me more than all philosophy or all history. It was on the closing day of the Paris Exhibition of 1867, when all the schools of the city were admitted free. At the exit from the building I was detained by the entrance of thousands of the pupils, male and

"If any one explains Christianity as an attempt to gratify boundless egotism on the basis of an arrangement by which one of the contracting parties, in return for deeds of self-renunciation and voluntary sufferings in this relatively brief and fleeting life, is to receive eternal life, he thus designates precisely the sole mode of contemplation which is possible to invincible human egotism, but by no means the disillusioned view held by those who actually practise voluntary self-sacrifice and submission to suffering. For, by such renunciation and suffering, egotism is practically abolished, so that whoever practises them

female, of the Paris schools, and remained an hour wrapped in the review of almost each individual in this youthful army that represented a whole future. The experience of this hour affected me so terribly that in my deep emotion I finally burst into tears and sobs. This was noticed by one of the nuns, who was, with touching care, conducting one of the processions of girls, and who at the entrance door ventured, as if by stealth, to look up. Her glance fell upon me for too short a time to give her, even under the most favorable circumstances, a conception of my condition, and yet, so versed and practised was I already in the art of Seeing, that in this glance I could recognize an ineffably beautiful solicitude as the soul of her life. The impression this vision created was all the deeper, as I nowhere else in the interminable throng saw any thing like or resembling it. On the contrary, every thing had filled me with horror and sorrow. I saw in prophetic outlines all the vices of the great capital, with its weakness, sickness, grossness, and greed, dulness and degradation of natural vivacity, fear and anguish, insolence and trickery. All this led on by teachers mostly belonging to religious orders in the hideous garb of fashionable priesthood, teachers themselves without wills, strict and stern, but rather obeying than ruling. Every thing soulless—except that one poor Sister.

"A long, deep silence revived me from the impression of that terrible Sight. To see and to be silent—these would be the elements of deliverance from this busy world."

Wagner concludes: "To speak of the things of this world seems to be very easy, because all the world speaks of them, but to present them so that they speak themselves is given to few."—*N. Y. Musical Courier.*

is thus really emancipated from all the ideas of Time and Space. Such an one can no longer seek any happiness lying in Time or Space, even though they were conceived to be eternal and illimitable. That which gives him superhuman strength to suffer voluntarily must be felt even by himself in the form of a deep inner happiness, unperceived by either himself or any one else, and wholly incommunicable to any one save by external earthly suffering. It must be a boundless, sublime, and blissful feeling of having overcome the world, compared with which the vain satisfaction of having conquered the world is childishly empty." ("Wagner," VII., p. 82.) "When, after severe illness, St. Francis again beheld the wonderful landscape of the surroundings of Assisi, he was asked how the spectacle pleased him, upon which the saint, lifting his gaze from the depths of the inner world in which he had been so profoundly absorbed, and fixing his eyes once more upon the external scene, replied : 'No longer as before.'"

Wagner looked for no immediate social reform. Apparently the *selfish* rich will continue to pursue their own ends, regardless of the continually deeper degradation of the degraded poor, until, at last, the accumulated mass of misery will swell above and overflow all the bulwarks of social order, in another of the revolutions in which all plutocracies find their end. Meanwhile, he writes :

"Let us then recognize, with the Redeemer in our heart, that it is not the deeds but the sufferings of men which bring *us near to them,* and make them worthy of our thoughts : that to the defeated hero, not to the victor, our sympathies belong. In all surrounding nature, in the violence of the elements, in the unalterable, self-asserting lower will, alike in sea and in desert, in the insect and in the worm on which we tread, we see manifested around and beneath us the enormous tragedy of earthly existence. As the spectacle overmasters our feelings, let us daily look to the Redeemer on the Cross as our last sublime refuge." ("Wagner," 1880, p. 296.)

To cease from worldly-mindedness is assuredly no light matter. Says Wagner :

"The greatest miracle for the natural man certainly is the conversion of the Will, in which event is involved a suspension of the laws of Nature itself. Whatever can effect this conversion must necessarily be sublimely supernatural and superhuman, and union with it becomes the one thing needful. This something the disciples were taught to call the Kingdom of God, in opposition to the kingdoms of this world. He who called to Himself the weary, the heavy-laden, the suffering, the meek, and the lovers of enemies, taught them that the all-loving was their Heavenly Father as whose Son He Himself was sent to them, His brethren. Here we see the greatest of miracles and call it Revelation." ("Wagner," 1880, p. 271.)

We have now followed Wagner to the end of life. What of the Beyond ? Wagner writes :

" If it be rational to assume that the certain de-struction of our globe is only a question of time, we shall have to accustom ourselves to think of the human race as doomed to extinction. But, then, *the matter may involve a destiny lying outside of time and space;* and the question whether or not the world has a moral significance, we may attempt to answer by asking ourselves how we propose to perish, like brutes or in a godlike manner ? " ("Wagner," 1881, p. 250.)

" In true religion there occurs a complete reversal of all those aims upon which the State is based and organized. The happiness which in that way is un-attainable, the soul abandons the effort to attain, in order by a diametrically opposite way to attain it. The truth dawns upon the religious consciousness that there must be another world besides this, because in this the inextinguishable craving for happiness is not to be stilled, and accordingly an-other world is required for our redemption. (VIII., 27.) What an indescribable gain would it be to those who, on the one hand, are terrified by the threats of ecclesiasticism, and on the other, are driven to despair by our men of physical science, if to the sublime edifice of Love, Faith, and Hope we could annex a distinct recognition of the ideality of this world, conditioned by the laws of Time and Space as at present the sole foundation of our perceptions ! For from the point of view of that ideality, all questions of the disquieted soul after a where and a when of the other world, will, nay, must be, answerable by a blissful smile. For if to these seemingly infinitely weighty questions there is any answer, it has been given by Schopenhauer with unequalled precision and beauty in these words: 'Peace, rest, and happiness dwell only where there is neither any where nor any when.' " (" Wagner," 1880, p. 339.)

Says Schopenhauer:

" Dying is certainly to be regarded as the real aim of life : in the moment of death all that is decided for which the whole course of life was only the preparation and the introduction." (" World as Will and Idea," Vol. III., p. 463.) " Abolish the concentration of consciousness in the brain by magnetic sleep, and our existence shows itself beyond our persons, and in other beings most strikingly by direct participation in the thoughts of another individual, and ultimately by the power of knowing the absent, the distant, and even the future, thus by a kind of omnipresence. I believe that at the moment of death we become conscious that it is a mere illusion that has limited our existence to our persons." (" World as Will and Idea," Vol. III., pp. 418, 419.)

With this we reach the end of our lecture. We have heard Wagner's assertion of the right of human nature to claim scientific recognition for both the spiritual intuitions and the spiritual inspirations of man ; we have heard his eloquent confession of the Divinity of Christ as at once Redeemer and Sole Refuge : we have heard his defence of religious

Dogma from the attacks of every-day common human reason : we have heard his denunciation of all ways by which selfishness exalts itself at the cost of plunging multitudes of fellow-creatures into continually deeper abysses of want and degradation ; and finally, we have heard his declaration of belief in another world of redemption. It only remains to ask how he was led to these doctrines.

In the passage cited at the beginning of this lecture from Dr. Newton's sermon, it was said that " All lines of true human thought focus in religion."

Wagner says :

" My thoughts upon these matters came to me as creative artist in my intercourse with the public. Having thus attained to the conviction that true art can thrive only upon the basis of a true morality, I could but recognize a proportionately higher mission for art, since I found true art to be at one with true religion. "   (" Wagner," 1880, p. 289.)

Do we ask the moral of Wagner's life ?

In 1851 Wagner wrote to Liszt :

" I have erred much in my artistic efforts, not being one of the elect who, like Mendelssohn, received the only true, infallible, solid food of art like Heavenly Manna in their mouths, and who therefore are able to say, ' I have never erred.' Only through error can we poor earthworms get to a knowledge of the truth, which, however, for that very reason, we love passionately like a bride whom we have won, instead of with the genteel approval with which we regard a spouse selected for us by our dear parents." *

Accordingly, we may say the moral of Wagner's life was: Accept, like Mendelssohn, and ye shall Have; but Seek, like Wagner, and ye shall Find. As Columbus once sought a more direct route to the already known Indies, and found a new world, so Wagner, seeking a higher type of musical drama, explored both myth and philosophy to their inmost depths, and discovered, beneath and above all, as sole foundation for a true Humanitarianism, the Logos, the Christ, the Son of the Living God.

On this discovery he placed an enduring seal.

In 1856 he wrote to Liszt of a "splendid subject" he meant to execute, entitled, "Victory, the most Perfect Salvation."

In 1872 he said to the writer of this lecture: "What a grand thing is youth! To youth all things are possible. I am now old; but I am not as old as some would like to have me. In three or four years I shall produce the Nibelung's Ring entire, *and then I shall bring out one more work!*"

In 1880 the "one more work" was really brought out at Baireuth. But then, in naming it, his mind seems

---

* It is a remarkable fact, that about thirty years after Wagner thus modestly classed himself among the earthworms, Mr. Darwin published his famous work on the "Formation of Vegetable Mould," in which he exhibits the earthworm as a "worker of vast geological changes, a planer down of mountain sides, and an ally of the Society for the Preservation of Ancient Monuments"; in a word, the main instrumentality, under Providence, for conserving the best things belonging to the past, by burying them out of sight, while providing for future generations the very soil whence their nutriment must be drawn!

to have reverted to a remarkable passage in St. Paul's
First Epistle to the Corinthians, where the expression
"foolishness" is dwelt upon with striking persistency:

"For the word of the cross to those indeed perish-
ing is foolishness, and to us—those being saved—it
is the power of God, for it hath been written, 'I
will destroy the wisdom of the wise, and the intelligence of the intelligent I will bring to nought';
where is the wise? where the scribe? where a dis-
puter of this age? Did not God make foolish the
wisdom of this world? For, seeing in the wisdom
of God the world through wisdom knew not God,
it did please God through the foolishness of preaching to save those believing. Since Jews ask a sign,
and Greeks seek wisdom, also we—we preach Christ
crucified, to Jews, indeed, a stumbling-block, and to
Greeks foolishness, and to those called—both Jews
and Greeks—Christ the power of God, and the wisdom of God, because the foolishness of God is wiser
than men, and the weakness of God is stronger than
men. . . . that no flesh may glory before Him.
. . . He who is glorying—in the Lord let him
glory."

And now,—Wagner having long since learned,
contrary to his former opinion, that the Christian
dare bring deeds to offer to his God—the name for
the "Victory, or the most Perfect Salvation" was
found. It was, Par-si-fal, which being interpreted,
is "Fool without Guile," or as St. Paul writes, "The
foolishness of God, which is wiser than men," namely,
"Christ crucified."

APPENDIX.

APPENDIX.

Note I.—"*That there is an ethical tendency in Wagner's works is clear.*"
—(P. 17.)

It has not escaped notice that, in the " Flying Dutchman," the heroine, Senta, illustrates the precept, " Greater love than this hath no one, that any one his life may lay down for his friends " ; that in " Tannhaueser," as the Rev. Mr. Haweis pointed out, we see contrasted the " Tremendous Empire of the Senses, and the Immense Supremacy of the Soul ! " that, in " Lohengrin," we have a parable of the human soul as typified by Elsa, who, after seeking supernatural aid, should have abode in faith and trust, saying : " I have known in whom I have believed, and have been persuaded that he is able that which I have committed to him to guard—to that day." [1]

It is not, however, so generally recognized that in " Tristan and Isolde," where neither a Swinburne, a Tennyson, nor even a Matthew Arnold discovered the possibility of any thing not involving a sinful intrigue, Wagner gives us two characters ideally created for each other, and whom King Mark would gladly have seen wedded, and, but for the jealousy of the nobles, actually seated on his throne, but whose fates are crossed by purely external circumstances and conventionalities, as well as in part by their own blindness before it was too late to redeem their fortunes. They are led to commit themselves to each other in the sight of suspicious observers at a moment when each one believes death imminent, and thenceforth meet but once, and then at the treacherous instigation of a false friend who induces them to meet in order that he may profit by betraying them. In that hour, swayed by the loftiest principles of honor, they exhibit a conversion of will such as Wagner has termed " the greatest of miracles for the natural man, since it involves a suspension of the laws of Nature, and hence whatever can effect it must be sublimely supernatural and superhuman." Accordingly, that to which the noble pair dedicate themselves is not any " earthly house," but a " house not made with hands—age-during—in the heavens . . . that

[1] A child of twelve years gave the following interpretation of " Lohengrin," after a first hearing : " There was an idea back of all they did on the stage. No one believes a man really came down a river in a boat drawn by a swan ; but Elsa prayed in trouble, and her prayer was answered. Lohengrin came to her aid like Christ, and they tried to kill him, and Elsa herself did not firmly believe in him, and so he went away and she died."

the mortal may be swallowed up of the life." Meanwhile, King Mark has, unknown either to his court or to the world, spared Isolde the misery of the consummation of a loveless marriage to himself, and has thus won her boundless filial devotion ; and when, by circumstances which, at the time, he himself cannot understand, he is placed before his court in the position of an injured husband, he becomes a royal embodiment of obedience to the command to " Judge not according to appearance, but the righteous judgment judge."

After the foregoing instances we are prepared to see in the " Master-Singers of Nuremburg," conventional art taught by the inspired artist, Walter, that " The letter doth kill, and the spirit doth make alive " ; while both Walter and Eva learn from Hans Sachs " From all appearance of evil abstain ye." We also understand the scene, by some deemed æsthetically unintelligible, in Rhine-Gold, where Alberich, to accumulate the golden hoard, " grinds the faces of the poor " until they are more brute than human, and almost too degraded and contemptible to evoke pity. In the same musical drama, the giants, Fafner and Fasolt, show that " Whoso is hasting to be rich is not acquitted " ; the thesis of the " Nibelung's Ring," in its entirety being, that greed of gain is fatal to all the ideal and innocent joys of life. In the " Valkyrie " we see, in the person of Brynhilda, the free impulse based on sympathy and unselfish love, which is the distinguished mark of Christianity, introduced in the midst of the fatalistic circle of gods and heroes ; Brynhilda's protecting flames reminding us of the promise in Zechariah, " I am to her a wall of fire round about." In " Siegfried," the seed of the woman, born in the dragon's cave, bruises the serpent's head ; and in the " Dooms-Day of the Gods," Love and Free Will, in the person of Brynhilda, triumph over paganism in the destruction of Walhalla, the slain Siegfried and Brynhilda being, in spite of Wagner's close superficial adherence to the traditional details of the legend of the Nibelungs, remarkably suggestive of the slain Lamb and His loving Bride the Church, which follows Him out of this world to the heavenly city. While, finally, in " Parsifal " we are reminded of the saying of the great Seer of Sweden : " Inasmuch as all things subsist from the Divine Principle, and all things thence derived must needs be representative of those things by which they had existence, it follows, that the visible universe is nothing but a theatre representation of the Lord's Kingdom, and this latter is a theatre representation of the Lord Himself."

NOTE II.—" *The feeblest myth is better than the strongest theory : myth recording a natural impression on the imaginations of great men and unpretending multitudes.*"—(P. 18.)

Herbert Spencer argues against the superiority of rational theories to natural impressions as follows :

" Reason has been instrumental in putting down forms of mental government—the government by prejudice, the government by tradition, etc. ; and *wherever it has replaced them tends to play the despot in their stead.* . . . By extinguishing other superstitions Reason makes itself the final object of superstition. In minds freed by its help from unwarranted beliefs, it becomes that to which an unwarranted amount of belief is given. . . . The remarkable fact is that this excessive confidence in Reason, as compared with the simpler modes of intellectual action, is not seen in those by whom Reason has been employed with such astonishing results. Men of science, now as in all past times, subordinate the deliverances of consciousness reached through mediate processes to the deliverances reached through immediate processes. . . . The chemist whose reasoned-out formula for a new compound implies that the separated precipitate put into his scales should weigh a grain, and who finds that it weighs two grains, at once abandons the verdict of his reasoning, and never dreams of calling in question the verdict of his direct perception. So it is with all classes of men whose joint efforts have brought our knowledge of the universe to its present coherent comprehensive state. It is rather among the spectators of these vast achievements of Reason that we find this exaggerated estimate of its powers ; and in the minds of these spectators its usurpation is often marked in proportion as their converse with Nature has been remote. . . . In describing the worship of that which puts down superstitions as in itself the final superstition, we come, indeed, much nearer to literal truth than at first appears. For this worship implies the assumption that by shaping consciousness into a particular form, there is given to it some power independent of the power which belongs intrinsically to its substance. . . . While it is impossible for Reason to prove its own superior trustworthiness, it is quite possible for it to prove its own inferior trustworthiness. Self-analysis shows that all its dicta being derivative, are necessarily less certain than those from which they are derived. . . . By its own account, it cannot possibly do more than compare and intercept the evidences which perception has given. So long as it limits itself to detecting incongruities among the evidences of perception, and finding out where they have arisen, Reason performs an all-important function ; but it exceeds its function, and commits suicide, when it concludes the evidence of perception to be *false in substance.* Reason can do nothing more than reconcile the testimonials of perception with one another. When it proved that the sun does not move round the earth, but that the earth turns on its axis, Reason substituted for an old interpretation which was irreconcilable with the various facts, a new interpretation which was reconcilable with them, while it equally well accounted for the more obvious facts. *But Reason did not question the existence of the Sun, the Earth, and their relative motion !*"—(" Principles of Psychology," 390, 391, 441.)

(Would that our men of physical science oftener took this ground in regard to religious dogmas as well, many of which represent the most ancient spiritual perceptions of mankind, and embody problems which can no more be ignored out of existence than Sun, Moon, or Earth !)

" In each sermon, I have passed quickly through the husks of popular dogmas, to find out and bring to you somewhat of that which I understand to be the inner substance of these doctrines ; seeking to show that, so far from representing exploded superstitions, these doctrines stand for most real problems ; problems which are still before us as they were before our fathers ; problems which we must state, as best we can, in the thought and language of our day, as our fathers stated them in the thought and language of their day ; or that, failing in any satisfactory statement, we must rest content in the old formulas, until the Divine Spirit causes 'the doctrine of knowledge to appear as the light.' I have thus sought to indicate to you that the old beliefs, when stripped of the glosses of the popular imagination, read far more nobly than most men dream ; and that we can see that they are capable of taking on still higher forms ; of which dim shadows fall athwart our path to-day, assuring us that there will be a theology of the future, in which the old doctrines shall quicken into beliefs full of power over life. Our wisdom, in this trying age, when change follows change in our mental outlook, is to bide patiently under the old forms, even when not satisfactory ; rejecting the follies and wrongs of the popular theology, but holding by the doctrines of which they are distorted images."—(Rev. R. Heber Newton, D.D., " Philistinism, or Plain Words Concerning Certain Forms of Modern Skepticism," Putnam's Sons, New York.)

" The theological thaw going on so rapidly all around us is one of *words only*, the truth remains unchanged."—(Spencer.)

NOTE III.—" *A spirit voice will say to you something real and thoroughly comprehensible, yet never before heard.*"—(P. 20.)

" At the side of the world, which we perceive by virtue of the functions of the waking brain, stands, as is corroborated in every one's experience by dreams, a second world quite equal to the first in distinctness . . . a world which as Object, cannot lie outside of us. . . . As the organ of dreams cannot be excited to activity by external impressions (against which the brain is then entirely closed) this excitation must occur by means of changes in the inner organism which manifest themselves to our waking consciousness only as obscure feelings. But it is through this inner life that we are allied to all nature, and thus partakers in the essential nature of things in such a way that the forms of external knowledge, Time and Space, are no longer to be applied to our relations with that nature ; whence Schopenhauer convincingly argues the origin of prophetic dreams which make the most distant things perceptible, and in extreme cases, the entrance of somnambulistic clairvoyance. . . . To this let us now add the other phenomenon of spirit-seeing ; and with reference to it as well, employ Schopenhauer's hypothetical explanation, according to which it is a clairvoyance which takes place while the brain is awake. . . . The shape which from the interior is projected before the eye, in no wise belongs to the real, phenomenal world ; it lives, nevertheless, before the spirit-seer, with all the characteristics of an actual being. With this projection before the waking person's eyes of the image beheld by the inner Will alone, let us compare Shakespeare's work, in order to explain him to ourselves as the spirit-seer and spirit-conjurer who was able, from his inner perception, to place the shapes of men of all times before his and our waking eyes in such a manner that they seem actually to live before us."—(Wagner's "Beethoven," G. Schirmer, N. Y.)

" The Abbe Trithemius, who in magic art was the master of Agrippa, explains in his 'Stenography' the secret of conjurations and evocations in an exceedingly natural and philosophical manner. To evoke a spirit, he says, is to enter into the ruling idea of that spirit, and if we rise morally higher in the same line, we shall draw that spirit after us and it will serve us."—(" The Mysteries of Magic," Waite.)

NOTE IV.—" *To the Goliath of Modern Science art daily becomes more and more of a mere rudiment of a former cognitive stage of human life.*"—(P. 23.)

" I have almost lost my taste for pictures or music. . . . My mind seems to have become a kind of machine for grinding general laws out of large collections of facts, but why this should have caused the atrophy of that part of the brain alone, on which the higher tastes depend, I cannot conceive. . . . If I had to live my life again, I would have made a rule to read some poetry and listen to some music at least once every week ; for perhaps the parts of my brain now atrophied would thus have been kept active through use. The loss of these tastes is a loss of happiness, and may possibly be injurious to the intellect, and more probably to the moral character, by enfeebling the emotional part of our nature."—(Charles Darwin, " Autobiography," i., pp. 101, 102.)

NOTE V.—" *True artistic productivity may all too easily induce a relapse into the 'inspiration-swindle' of surmounted periods of culture !*"—(P. 24.)

" Savants, who are only savants, have been able to deny God. That can be conceived of, for when the heart does not communicate to the brain its generous burnings which illumine and fecundate ; when it does not inflame those intuitions which constitute genius, the mind cannot go very far. From that comes the cold reasoning condemned to a profound sterility, that dryness of perception and narrowness of vision which explain in some sort the atheism which certain savants profess. But for any artist to deny God, God the cause, the beginning and the end of his art, *God the source of his inspirations and his genius,*—let us say it without fear of contradiction, let us proclaim it to the eternal honor of art, never has such a monstrosity been produced. No, never! Never has an artist denied his God. For him, art is a magnificent objective upon whose field appears an entire transluminous world, and to whose visions he incessantly tends to unite himself. For him, art is still a mystic fountain from which escapes a celestial perfume and across which he feels, he sees, he touches in some sort that God who fills him with irrepressible raptures.

"If you own one of those costly instruments called telescopes, why do you value it? Is it not because of the property it possesses of showing to your surprised eyes vast and profound perspectives invisible without its aid? It is, then, the astounding views brought within the range of your vision that you love the instrument for; certainly you would not say you loved the telescope for the telescope! Now art is the telescope of a supernatural world. Love art for art! What does that mean? It is idolatry. It is to love the portrait of a friend not for the friend, but for a portrait; to love an image for the image, not for what it represents! In art one must love something besides art if one would know how to love art! True art purifies the life, illumines the mind, makes perfect and sanctifies the soul, and transfigures it to identity with things divine."—(Francis Delsarte.)

NOTE VI.—"*Instead of worshipping the true Jehovah, who rejoices within the hearts of men when they kill their animal passions and sacrifice to Him their erroneous opinions, they created a bloodthirsty God whom they called Jehovah.*"—(P. 27.)

Sanconiatho, B.C. 1000, gives the origin of human sacrifices thus: "It was the custom among the ancients in times of great calamity, in order to prevent the ruin of all, for the rulers of the city or the nation to sacrifice to the avenging deity the most beloved of their children as the price of redemption. For the Supreme God Il had an only son whom once, when great danger beset the land, he offered up as a sacrifice to Heaven." ("Assyria," by Ragozin, chap. v., Putnam's Sons.) *

* Both the natural parental shrinking of the ancients from the sacrifice of their offspring and the lengths to which they could summon up resolution to go in their efforts to propitiate the avenging power to which the supreme god Il had sacrificed his only son, is shown by an occurrence in the history of the Carthaginians, who having been beaten in a very important battle, made a severe investigation, which showed that the city nobles had for some time purchased and fattened low-born children and substituted these for their own children in the sacrifices. To this impiety the anger of the god was attributed, and a national expiatory sacrifice was ordered on a large scale: two hundred boys of the noblest

In the oldest writings known to us, except perhaps the Book of Job, namely, those of the Shumiro-Accads, who dwelt between the Tigris and the Euphrates rivers, above the Persian Gulf, the sign of a star is used to express the idea of the divine principle. The Semitic language of Babylonia read the sign of the star, Ilu, god. This word Ilu or El we find in all Semitic languages, ancient and modern, in the name given to God in the Arabic Allah, as well as in the Hebrew Elohim. ("The Story of Chaldea," Ragozin, chap. v., Putnam's Sons.)

In the Hebrew Scriptures, the name El, or Al, occurs in various forms and combinations, thus: "In the beginning of Elohim's preparing the heavens and the earth—the earth hath existed waste and void, and darkness is on the face of the deep, and the Spirit of Elohim * fluttering on the face of the waters, and Elohim saith, Let light be, and light is."—(Genesis i., 1-3.) "And the sons of Elohim see the daughters of men (Adam) that they are fair . . . and they have borne to them—they are the heroes, who, from old, are the men of name."—(Genesis vi., 2-4.) "And Melchizedek king of Salem hath brought out bread and wine, and he is priest of El."— (Genesis xiv., 18.) "I am El Shaddai,† walk habitually before Me . . . and I will give My covenant between Me and thee, and multiply thee exceedingly."—(Genesis xvii., 1, 2.) "Lo, I am seeing four men loose, walking in the midst of fire, and they have no hurt; and the appearance of the fourth is like to a son of Elah."—(Daniel iii., 25.) "Wizards who chatter and mutter, Doth not a people seek unto its Elohim?" ‡—(Isaiah viii., 19.) "Lo, the Virgin is conceiving, and is bringing forth a son, and hath called his name Immanu-el."—(Isaiah vii., 14.) "No Eloah of any nation and kingdom is able to deliver his people from my hand."—(Sennacherib against

---

ruling families perished, and many of their parents voluntarily sacrificed their own lives at the same time.—(Ragozin's "Assyria.")

The Old Testament contains numerous allusions to similar sacrifices. Thus of the king of Moab we read: "The Israelites rose and smote the Moabites so that they fled before them; and they went forward into the land smiting the Moabites. . . . Then the king of Moab took his eldest son that should have reigned in his place and offered him for a burnt offering upon the wall. *And there came great wrath upon Israel, and they departed from him and returned to their own land.*" (This occurred about 850 B.C. —See 2 Kings, iii., 24-27.)

The Jews themselves had a place outside the walls of Jerusalem, the valley of Tophet, where sacrificial pyres were constantly kept blazing and were often fed with child-victims. —(Jeremiah vii., 30, 31; xix., 5-7.)

* Elohim is a plural formed from a feminine singular (Eloh) by adding the usual termination of the masculine plural (im). "And Elohim prepareth the man in His image, in the image of Elohim He prepareth him, a male and a female He prepared them."—(Genesis i., 27.)

† Shaddai, *i. e.*, El of the breast, the nourisher, obviously related to the many-breasted Diana of the Ephesians.

‡ *I. e.*, to its mighty dead.

Hezekiah ; 2 Chronicles xxxii., 15.) "And Saul sweareth to her by Jehovah, saying, Jehovah liveth, punishment doth not meet thee for this thing. And the woman saith, Whom do I bring up to thee? and he saith, Samuel —bring up to me. And the woman seeth Samuel. . . . And the king saith to her . . . what hast thou seen? and the woman saith unto Saul, Elohim have I seen coming up out of the earth. And he saith to her, What is his form? and she saith, An aged man is coming up, and he is covered with an upper robe ; and Saul knoweth he is Samuel."—(1 Samuel xxviii., 10–14.)

The incommunicable name Jehovah, which stands over against Elohim in the preceding passage, is variously derived from roots signifying, respectively, He who exists, He who causes, and He who causes (rain, lightning, heavenly bodies) to fall. Thus : "And the day is, that sons of Elohim come in to station themselves by Jehovah, and there doth come also the Hater (Satan) in their midst. . . . And Jehovah saith to the Hater, Lo, all that he hath is in thine hand. . . . While this one is speaking another also hath come and saith, 'Fire of Elohim' [the star] hath fallen from the heavens. . . . And Job riseth . . . and he saith . . . Jehovah hath given and Jehovah hath taken : let the name of Jehovah be blessed."—(Job i., 6–21.)

We believe that we shall not err if, in the Scriptural distinction between Jehovah and Elohim, we perceive, on the one hand, in Jehovah, God objectively conceived, God as Transcendent above His Creation ; and on the other hand, in El, Elah, Eloah, Elohim, El Shaddai, etc., we perceive God subjectively conceived, God as Immanent in His World, and particularly in the great men and other intelligences through whose instrumentality the destinies of nations, races, mankind at large, nay, even that of planets themselves, are wrought out.

Modern metaphysics render such a view easy of comprehension. Whoever has learned from Spencer to view the antithetical conceptions of Spirit and Matter as rendered necessary to us only through the relation of subject and object, while Spirit no less than Matter is regarded as but a sign of an underlying Reality, must find it but natural to view the antithetical conceptions in Holy Scripture of God Transcendent and God Immanent, Jehovah and Elohim, as also rendered necessary only through the same relation of subject and object, both Jehovah and Elohim being regarded as signs of the underlying Unity. To that which underlies Spirit and Matter Spencer gives the name of the Unknowable Reality ; to Him who appears to us in the Old Testament now as Elohim and anon as Jehovah, English translations of the Bible give the names of Lord and God. As Elohim, or God Immanent, obviously is the heart of creation, not fashioning things from without, but instead evolving all things from within, in placing Elohim at the very beginning of Genesis, the Old Testament may be said to take Evolution for granted from the very outset, and to meet the demands of modern thought still further by its recognition of the fundamental antithesis of subject and object in representing the one God now as Elohim or God Immanent, and again as Jehovah or God Transcendental. Hence it would seem that Spencer himself must eventually reach the conclusion, that if God be Unknowable to man, this can be true of Him only as Jehovah or God Transcendental ; while as Elohim, or God Immanent in His World, this " God Unknown . . . who did make the world and all things in it . . . giving to all life and breath . . . is not far from each one of us, for in Him we live, and move, and are " ; being Him of whom (according to certain ancient poets) " we also are offspring " ; the Lord of the conscience ; and the " Divinity " (according to a more modern poet) "that shapes our ends, rough hew them how we may."

The idea of God which is thus developed is represented in the emblem known as Solomon's Seal. In it the Evolution of matter upward toward spirit is symbolized by a triangle resting on its base, $\triangle$ the three sides of which represent the " Three who are testifying in the earth, the Spirit and the water and the blood " ; while the Involution of spirit into matter is symbolized by an inverted triangle, ∇ the three sides of which represent the " Three who are testifying in the heaven, the Father, the Word, and the Holy Spirit " ; The latter three, who " are one," and the former three, who " are into the one," form when combined the six-pointed star so prominent among ecclesiastical symbols, reminding us at once of the ancient Assyrian sign of divinity in general, and also of the star which at the birth of Emmanu-el was seen of the magi in the east and stood over where the child lay.

The account given by Sanconiatho of the sacrifice of his only son by the supreme god Il when danger beset the land, plainly connects Il with the gods and heroes of earth, and satisfactorily explains, if not, as he supposes, the *origin* of human sacrifices, at least the reason for their perpetuation. We have, however, in our day, seen no less a scholar than F. Max Müller, affirm * of the Polynesian story of the destruction of sky-supporting Ru, whose bones came tumbling down and were shivered on the earth into countless fragments of pumice-stone, which are scattered over every hill and valley of Mangaia, to the very edge of the sea ; that " this tearing asunder of heaven and earth was originally no more than a description of what might be seen every morning when, after a dark night, the sun of the morning appeared, the dawn was hurled away, and the sky seen lifted high above the earth." (Prof. Müller admits, however, that " Why pumice-stone should be called the bones of Ru, [*i.e.*, the Dawn,] we cannot tell, *without knowing a great deal more of the language of Mangaia than we do at present*" *!*) If a great modern authority can soberly offer such an interpretation of a story

* India : What can it teach us ?, Lecture V.

manifestly relating to the supreme catastrophe of history, myth, and legend, (see Note XXII.), we may be pardoned for not accepting literally the statement of Sanconiatho, and for preferring instead to draw from it the conclusion that human sacrifices originated in a gross, materialistic misconception of a primitive doctrine of sacrifice dating from the time of the great catastrophe in the solar system to which reference has been made.

By the Hebrew priests clearly the history and meaning of the sacrifice made by Il were understood and perpetuated in a way which kept their followers closely in sympathy with the ideas on which were based the atrocities of the worship of surrounding nations; whence we understand the continual lapses of the Hebrew people into the worship of Baal, Moloch, etc., in which worship they may have felt that they found the original of which their own was a copy. By the Hebrew prophets, however, obviously the sacrifice made by El was understood in a totally different and purely spiritual way; for they declare explicitly that the " Sacrifices of Elohim are a broken spirit, a heart broken and bruised,"—(Psalm li., 17.)

From this point of view, the doctrine of the sacrifice of his only son by the supreme god El is a witness, from the time of a catastrophe which may be outlined from, if indeed it be not actually symbolized for us in, the Book of Job, of the " Natural law of sacrifice which runs through all creation and is the expression of the very heart of God himself ; under which law men are lifted into the human life divine, as men are ready to sacrifice everything, even to life itself, in the vicariousness of love whose perfect manifestation is Jesus Christ " ; the foundation of the doctrine being belief in the existence of a Power (to use the words of the Rev. Dr. Parkhurst, of New York City) " who is the most tremendously obligated Being in the universe," and who meets His obligations to the uttermost in behalf of all who will hearken unto His voice and walk in His ways.

In the light of the foregoing facts of etymology, and history, sacred and profane, it is significant that not only was our Lord's ministry mainly associated with the services of the synagogues, which thus became the rallying points for the primitive Christian congregations, the whole influence of His ministry being to put an end to the bloody rites of the Temple ; but what is even more to the point, He distinctly connected His Being and Mission with the great event of which only a dim shadow survives in Sanconiatho's account of the deed of Il whence human sacrifices originated ; and the New Testament writers and early Fathers supply further links which seem to turn the fabric from a chain into mail-armor.

Thus, if Sanconiatho tells us that once when danger beset the land the Supreme God Il sacrificed his only son ; the New Testament says that our Lord was truly Emanu-el, that is El with us. Of the time when, according to Sanconiatho, danger beset the land, He who was seen in Patmos with the seven stars in His right hand, elsewhere affirmed : " I was beholding Satan falling like lightning from the heavens." He further reminded Nicodemus (who as a master in Israel should have known these things), that *God (Theos, i. e.,* Dyaus, the shining one, identical with El), *did so love the world that His Son—the only begotten—He gave that every one believing in Him may not perish, but may have life age-during. For God did not send His Son to the world that he may judge the world, but that the world may be saved through Him.*

Again, in the agony of His death-throes upon the cross, just before He gave up the ghost, He cried with a loud voice, not to Jehovah, but instead to the Supreme God El ; " Eli, Eli, lama Sabachthani,"—El, El, why didst Thou forsake me !

Most fittingly, then, when the " Lamb slain from the foundation of the world" appeared to His disciples after the crucifixion,—He asked : " Was it not behoving the Christ these things to suffer?" *

The Christian Church has ever loved to see the Redeemer's form in the mysterious Melchizedek, King of Jerusalem and King of Peace, as also in other divine manifestations recorded in the Old Testament. Hence we may come to understand the profound meaning of the learned St. Augustine, when he writes :

" That in our times is called the Christian religion, which to know and to follow is the most sure and certain health, called according to that name, but not according to the thing itself of which it is the name, for the thing itself which is now called the Christian religion really was known to the ancients, nor was wanting at any time from the beginning of the human race until the time when Christ came in the flesh, from whence the true religion, which had previously existed, began to be called Christian ; and this in our days is the Christian religion, not as having been wanting in former times, but as having in later times received that name."—(" Opera Augustini," vol. i., p. 12.)

According to this, heathenism would represent a corruption of the original doctrine, while the truth as it is in Jesus would be the ancient doctrine restored to mankind by the Incarnation and Precious Death of Christ. Human and other sacrifices originated in a misapprehension of the spiritual

---

* Scorn and contumely and the cries of an angry crowd surround that altar on which the Son of God makes oblation of Himself ; and cross after cross strews the long Via Dolorosa of the narrow path that leadeth unto Life.

The wrongs of others wound the Son of God, and the stripes of others fall on His flesh. He is smitten with the pain of all creatures, and His heart is pierced with their wounds. There is no offence done and he suffers not, nor any wrong, and he is not hurt thereby. For his heart is in the breast of every creature and his blood in the veins of all flesh.

And inasmuch as a man loves and succours and saves even the least of God's creatures, he ministers unto the Lord.—(Kingsford.)

meaning of the primitive doctrine of the sacrifice by the Supreme God II of
His only Son to save the world.

> " Now let our souls on wings sublime
> Rise from the vanities of time,
> Draw back the parting veil and see
> The glories of eternity."

NOTE VII.—"*Materialistic physical science is destructive of Deism only,
while Christian theism is wholly beyond its reach.*"—(P. 29.)

The celebrated contention between Herbert Spencer and Frederick Harrison, touching " The Nature and Reality of Religion," was purely on the
plane of Theism. Mr. Spencer who, in the opinion of competent authorities,
possesses perhaps the grandest intellect which has appeared in philosophy in
two thousand years, summed up a paper entitled " Religion, a Retrospect
and Prospect," by saying : " The final outcome of that speculation commenced by primitive man, is that the Power manifested throughout the
Universe distinguished as material, is the same Power which in ourselves
wells up under the form of consciousness." Mr. Harrison, who is admit-
tedly one of the most brilliant of modern critics and essayists, followed up
Spencer's paper with one entitled " The Ghost of Religion," in which he
affirmed that to him, Spencer's paper seemed frankly unanswerable as a sum-
mary of philosophical conclusions on the theological problem ; but Harrison
objects that there is no religion in the consciousness of being " ever in the
presence of an Infinite and Eternal Energy, from which all things proceed."
Religion, says Harrison, must be anthropomorphic to be a working reality, and he claims that " the future will have to return to the Knowable, to
the religion of Realism, the religion of Humanity, as the grandest object of
reverence within the region of the real and known." " You can have no
religion," writes Harrison, " without kinship, sympathy, relation of some
kind between the believer, worshipper, servant, and the object of his belief."
To this Spencer rejoined, that as religion began, historically, with the worship of dead men, followed by that of ghosts continually less human and
more superhuman in attributes, to be told now that there is coming an era in
which the Universal Power men have come to believe in, will be ignored, and
human individualities, regarded now singly and now in their aggregate, will
again be the objects of religious feeling,—this is Retrogressive Religion."
" A spectator," says Mr. Spencer, " who, seeing a bubble floating on a great
river, had his attention so absorbed by the bubble that he ignored the river
out of which the bubble arose .   .   .   would fitly typify a disciple of M.
Comte, who centreing all his higher sentiments on Humanity, holds it absurd
to let either thought or feeling be occupied with that great stream of Creative Power .   .   .   of which Humanity is a transitory product."

From this point on, no advance was made in the debate. Harrison continued to see the need of relation of some kind between the worshipper and the object of his belief ; while Spencer continued to be conscious of the existence of a Superhuman Power unreached by the deepest analyses of matter, motion and thought and feeling, which will hereafter continue to be, under its transfigured form, an object of religious sentiment, a Power which, far from dwelling apart from man and the world, like the God of Deism, "is manifested through man and the world from instant to instant." Yet neither of the combatants could name the name of the Christ, the Mediator between the Unknowable and Humanity, though this name held the key to the situation, so that, if Spencer had named it, he must have won the case by holding his own and showing that with it he also possessed what Harrison insisted upon as essential ! The precise position of the *Logos* doctrine between Theism and Humanitarianism may be seen from the following citations :

" As the heart of God the Father, the Son of God is at the same time the heart of the world, through whom the Divine Light streams into creation. As the Logos of the Father, He is at the same time the eternal Logos of the world, through whom the Divine Light shines into creation. He is the ground and source of all reason in the creation, be it in men or angels, in Greek or Jew. He is the principle of the law and promises under the Old Testament, the eternal light which shines in the darkness of heathenism ; and all the holy grains of truth which are found in heathenism were sowed by the Son of God in the souls of men. . . . It was the Divine Logos Himself who imaged Himself beforehand in elect sons of men under the Old Covenant, who moulded human personalities to a limited extent after His own holy nature, and thus realized beforehand some features of the image whose entire Divine and human fulness He purposed to express in His revelation as the Christ. Nay, more *in the sons of the gods of heathendom*, and in the men who stood forward as witnesses of a noble, God-related humanity, *we may trace individual features of His image*, which He stamped on them, although the heathen misapprehended them, and did not lay hold on the promise they contained."—(Bishop Martensen, " Christian Dogmatics.")

" Christ is the Word of whom the entire human race are partakers ; those who live according to reason are Christians, though accounted atheists, while those who live without reason are enemies to Christ ; each man of the heathen writers spoke well in proportion to the share of the Word of God he had in him."—(Justin Martyr.)

" The Son of God is never displaced ; not being divided, not severed, not passing from place to place ; being always everywhere, and being contained nowhere ; complete mind, the complete paternal light. Christ is called Wisdom by the prophets. This is he who is the teacher of all created beings, the fellow-counsellor of God, who foreknew all things. There was always a natural manifestation of the one Almighty God among all right-thinking men. He whom we call Savior and Lord gave philosophy to the Greeks. He has dispensed His beneficence both to Greeks and to Barbarians. For the image of God is His Word, the genuine Son of Mind, the Divine Word, the archetypal light of light."—(Clement of Alexandria.)

"Concerning which salvation seek out and search out did prophets . . . searching in regard to what manner of time *the Spirit of Christ that was in them* was manifesting, testifying beforehand the sufferings of Christ and the glory after these."—(1 Peter i., 11.)

"Jesus answered them, Is it not having been written in your law; I said, ye are gods? If then he did call them gods unto whom the word of God came, (and the writing is not able to be broken,) of him whom the Father did sanctify, and send into the world, do ye say—Thou speakest evil, because I said, Son of God I am?"—(John x., 34–36.)

"As many as did receive Him, to them gave He authority to become sons of God."—(John i., 12.)

"There may be observed in the synchronizing of the history of faiths a remarkable tidal wave of intensity which seems acutely to affect the race, physically and mentally, and with remarkable regularity every 600 to 650 years, reminding us of the Sothic and other cycles, but especially of the mystical Phœnix or solar eras of Egypt and the East.

B.C.	3500	Egyptian Sacred Ritual.
	3000	Zoroaster (Bunsen).
	2500 } 2250 }	Flood, Tower of Babel.
	1750 } 1700 }	Exodus, Hindo Veda, Zend Avesta.
	1200 } 1100 }	King David, Hebrew Psalms.
	600	Buddha, Chinese Sacred Books.
	0	Jesus Christ.
A.D.	600	Mahomet, the Koran.
	1100	Crusades.
	1500 } 1600 }	Luther, Protestant Bible.

—(Forlong: "Chart of Rivers of Life.")

" 'Five hundred years, Ananda,' said Buddha in the 'Culavagga,' 'will the doctrine of the truth abide.' He also prophesied that a new Buddha (*i. e.*, 'Divine Intelligence') would come. 'He shall be the last to obtain the great spiritual light; and he will become a Lord called the "Buddha of Brotherly Love." ("Saddharma Pundarika.") Buddha died 470 B.C., so exactly 500 years after his death, the Buddha of Brotherly Love began to preach.'"*—(Arthur Lillie: "Buddhism in Christendom," title-page and preface, p. vii.)

"And all things are of God, who hath reconciled us to Himself by Jesus Christ and hath given to us the ministry of reconciliation."

"Interest in missions is no longer confined to the Christian Church. It has spread in all directions, and is encountered where least of all we have hitherto been accustomed to look for it. Twenty-five years ago a serious editorial in a great secular journal would have been a newspaper eccentricity. In the last five years we have learned from the secular press almost as much of the theology and success of missionary enterprise as from the religious.

"It is to this interest that the once universal belief that those who never hear of Christ are doomed to an endless hell, which belief was regarded as the prime motive of gifts to missions, is no longer a universal belief, and is no longer urged as a motive for sending missionaries to heathen lands. It is feared in some quarters, if it is admitted that the heathen are not inevitably doomed, the enthusiasm for missionary enterprise will pass away. This fear is not a secret. As a consequence, we are all more or less aware of the changes which time, reason, and a better knowledge of God's Word and of heathen religions have wrought in the Church's spirit as it bends itself to do what it knows it ought to do in extending the knowledge of Jesus Christ. Let us admit the truth, not grudgingly, but gladly. We do not send missionaries to rescue heathen from hell; we send them out to bring the heathen to a knowledge of God as revealed in Jesus.

"St. Paul's training, his interest in Jewish theology and the Jewish Church, his knowledge of his people, his wish to do something for them, did not fall in pieces when Jesus met him on his way to Damascus, but it got a new significance. Henceforth he was to go up and down the world, not to persecute people who were trying to find God and to serve Him by methods different from His own, but to declare to people who were seeking after God that He was not far from any one of them, and to make the altar to an unknown God burn with a sacrifice to the God whom Jesus had revealed.

* The main position of writers like Dr. Oldenburg is that the atheistic literature of Ceylon represents the earliest Buddhism, the Buddhism of the Little Vehicle. Hwen Ohsang contradicts this in toto. "In Ceylon," he says, "are about ten thousand monks who follow the doctrines of the Great Vehicle." He says, moreover, the controversy raged fiercely for a long time before the Great Vehicle was successful over the Little Vehicle. Yet even in Ceylon, the hotbed of the innovating school of Buddhism that dethroned God and demolished heaven, Buddha is yet worshipped, though as a non-God. Flowers are flung daily at this non-God. Morning and evening meals are proffered to him. Daily the non-God is asked to forgive sins. The mock Mohatmas that the notorious Mme. Blavatski professed to be in communication with also affirmed that there was no God. Upon all these atheistic Buddhists of the Great Vehicle, those of the Little Vehicle, who represent ancient Buddhism, composed a neat sarcasm. They called that Great Vehicle, Sunya Pushpa (the vehicle that drives to Nowhere).—(Arthur Lillie, "Buddhism in Christendom," pp. 218-221.)

" St. Paul goes on to tell how the old things become new, which is by our reconciliation to God. This brings not religion, but Christianity, squarely to the front. In these later times, when all there is of every thing clear round the earth has been brought to our notice and knowledge, it has been suggested that religion was not limited to Christianity ; that, for instance, Buddhism may make its contribution and Mohammedanism do its share. This suggestion does not frighten or puzzle us as once it did. When we were children Buddhism and Mahommedanism were regarded as unmixedly evil, but we don't think of them in that way now. We have come to hope that every religion may have something of value in it, and that that very element of value may be the door through which the truth of God is at last to enter.

" But along with this larger view has travelled the idea that one religion is as good as another, and that the Church of America has its hands full at home. Here exactly is our point. We know how truly Jesus has completed our own knowledge of the nature of good ; therefore we pray and give that all the world may have what we know and the peace which accompanies it. I cannot believe that Buddha has done for a single pagan what Christ has done for me. Therefore I stand here to speak for the agency which is sending Christ's message to the world."—(Rev. E. Winchester Donald, D.D.)

NOTE VIII.—" *An angry and vindictive God.*"—(P. 29.)

" . . . God spake in His word according to appearances ; as when it is said that He is angry, that He avenges, that He tempts, that He punishes, that He casts into Hell, that He condemns, yea, that He does evil ; while the truth is that God never is angry with any one, that He never avenges, tempts, punishes, casts into hell, or condemns. Such things are as far from God, nay, infinitely farther, than hell is from heaven. They are forms of speech then, used only according to the appearances. . . . Infernal fire comes from the same origin as heavenly fire, namely, from the sun of heaven, or the Lord ; but it is made infernal by those who receive it. For all influx from the spiritual world varies according to reception, or according to the forms into which it flows ; not differently from the heat and light from the sun of the world. The heat flowing thence into plantations and gardens produces vegetation, and also brings forth grateful and delicious odors ; and the same heat flowing into excrementitious and cadaverous substances produces putrefaction, and draws forth noisome and disgusting stenches. It is the same with the heat and light from the sun of heaven, which is love. When the heat or love thence flows into goods,—as in good men and spirits,—it renders their goods fruitful ; but when it flows into the wicked it produces a contrary effect, for their evils either suffocate or pervert it. So with the light of heaven ; (on the one hand) it gives intelligence and wisdom ; but (on the other hand) it is turned into insanities and fantasies of various kinds.

" ' There is none besides Me, I am Jehovah, there is none else, forming light and preparing darkness, making peace, and preparing evil, I am Jehovah, doing all these things.' (Isaiah, xlv., 4, 5.) A man who is in evil is bound to hell, and even as to his spirit, is actually there ; and after death he desires nothing more than to be where his evil is. A man therefore casts himself into hell after death, and not the Lord."—(Swedenborg.)

NOTE IX.—" *The God who was then and for the first time revealed to mankind.*"—(P. 31.)

" There exists an immense fact, equally appreciable by faith and by science, a fact which renders God in a certain sense visible on earth, an incontestable fact, and one of immense significance ; it is the manifestation in the world, from the epoch of the Christian revelation, of a spirit unknown to the ancients, a spirit evidently divine, more positive than science in its works, more magnificently ideal in its aspirations than the highest poetry, a spirit for which it has been necessary to create a new name, wholly unheard of in the sanctuaries of antiquity, and which in religion, both for science and for faith, is the expression of the absolute. This word is Charity, and the spirit of which we speak is called the spirit of charity, which is God in His earthly manifestation. Before charity, faith prostrates itself, and science bows down, overcome, for it is evidently something greater than humanity ; it is stronger than all passions, it triumphs over suffering and death ; it reveals Deity to every heart, and seems already to fill eternity by that realization of its legitimate hopes which it commences here below. By the spirit of charity, Jesus, expiring on the cross, triumphed over the anguish of the most frightful torments ; by the spirit of charity twelve artisans of Galilee conquered the world ; it is by charity, in fine, that the folly of the cross has become the wisdom of the nations, because all noble hearts have felt it a more sublime and worthy thing to believe with those who love and sacrifice themselves, than to doubt with the egotists and slaves of self-indulgence !"—(Alphonse Louis Constant in the " Mysteries of Magic," by Waite.)

NOTE X.—" *This confusion of thought is so great that it is really astonishing to see how the most important minds of all times, since the appearance of the Bible, have been cramped by it and betrayed into weakness of judgment.*"—(P. 31.)

In view of Wagner's antipathy towards the Jewish Old Testament and the Jewish race,—not however toward the latter in their individual capacity, for he had many distinguished friends and warm admirers among the Jewish people, from Carl Tausig, the inventor of the plan of Wagner Societies, by which the Baireuth performances were rendered financially possible, down to private connoisseurs,—it is curious to note that he himself, as a Saxon, may have been an Israelite, or a descendant of Israel, though not a Jew, or a descendant of Judah. The historical data are as follows: When Tiglath-Pileser carried the Ten Tribes of Israel into captivity, he called them in a monumental inscription, a copy of which is in the British Museum, the people of the land of Beth-Khumri. These Khumri, called sometimes the Gimiri, were known to the Greeks as Cimmeroi, and to the Romans as Cimbri. The Crimea is believed to have been called after them, and many Israelitish tombstones have been found there. According to Rawlinson, the ethnic name of Gimiri occurs in the cuneiform records as the Semitic equivalent of the Aryan name Saki. The Sacoe Scythians were termed the Gimiri by their Semitic neighbors. The Anglo-Saxons were a Teutonic, *i. e.,* a Gothic or Scythian tribe. They gave to the most fertile part of Armenia the name of Sakasena (Saxonia). These Sakai were called in their own country shortly before their captivity (*i. e.,* in Samaria) Beth-Isaac, the oriental pronunciation of the latter name being with the emphasis on the last syllable, I—*saac.* (The Danes, Normans, Jutes, Frisians, Welsh, etc., are descended from the same primitive race as the Anglo-Saxons.) From this point of view certain noteworthy features of the Reformation in England are strikingly suggestive of a vivid revival of race self-consciousness; as, for example, the extraordinary revival of Bible, and especially Old Testament, reading and study; the partiality for Hebrew names in baptism, and the instinctive fondness for the science of genealogy. ("We all had our genealogies. No other nation had this science as had the Jews; for all our land belonged to families, and the scribes kept a record of the boundaries of every piece of land, so that if it were sold, it should return to the same house at the end of fifty years."—"Life and Times of Jesus," James Freeman Clarke.) In view of Old Testament prophecies, such as that of Amos: "I destroy not utterly the house of Jacob. . . . I have shaken among all the nations the house of Israel, as one who doth shake with a sieve, and there falleth not a grain to the earth;" and that in Genesis concerning Ephraim (*i. e.,* the Israelites or lost tribes, not the Jews or children of Judah), "his seed is the fulness of the nations"; and their apparent present fulfilment in the supremacy of the Saxon (Teutonic) race in England, America, and Germany, it is to be regretted that Wagner should never have had disclosed to him any path of approach to the Old Testament which would have softened his asperity towards those venerable writings and the race forever historically identified with them.

(See "Our Race," by Lieut. C. A. L. Totten, U. S. A., "Our Race" Publishing Co., New Haven, Conn.)

NOTE XI.—"*The continual prosecution of physical experiments in the field of natural science has again led the ruling human intellect of the day to the conclusion that there is no God at all, but only force and matter.*"—(P. 31.)

The inventor Thomas A. Edison is obviously an exception to the above rule. In a recent talk to a newspaper reporter, he said: "I do not believe that matter is inert, acted on by outside forces. To me it seems that every atom is possessed by a certain amount of primitive intelligence. Look at the thousand ways in which atoms of hydrogen combine with those of other elements having a most diverse substance. Do you mean to say that they do this without intelligence? Atoms in harmonious and beautiful relations assume a beautiful order, interesting shapes and colors, or give forth a pleasant perfume as if expressing their satisfaction. In sickness, death, decomposition, or filth, the disagreement of the atoms immediately makes itself felt by bad odors. Gathered together in certain forms, the atoms constitute animals of the lower orders. Finally, they combine in man, who represents the total intelligence of all the atoms." "But where does this intelligence come from?" asked the reporter. "From some Power greater than ourselves," responded Mr. Edison. "Do you believe then in an intelligent Creator and personal God?" "Certainly," said Mr. Edison. "The existence of such a God can to my mind almost be proved from chemistry."

Herbert Spencer's Doctrine of the Unknowable:

"Matter, Motion, and Force, are but symbols of the Unknown Reality. A Power of which the nature remains forever inconceivable and to which no limits in Time or Space can be imagined, works in us certain effects. . . . Every voluntary act yields to the primitive man proof of a source of energy within him. . . . When producing motion in his limbs, and through them in other things, he is aware of the accompanying feeling of effort. And this sense of effort, which is the perceived antecedent of changes produced by him, furnishes him with a term of thought by which to represent the genesis of these objective changes. . . . That internal energy which in the experiences of the primitive man was always the immediate antecedent of changes wrought by him, . . . is the same energy which, freed from anthropomorphic accompaniments, is now figured as the cause of all external phenomena. . . . Consequently, the final outcome of that speculation commenced by primitive man, is that the Power manifested throughout the Universe distinguished as material, is the same Power which in ourselves wells up under the form of consciousness. . . . The ultimate form of the religious consciousness is the final development of a consciousness which at the outset contained a germ of truth obscured by multitudinous errors. . . . So far from regarding that which transcends phenomena as 'The All-Nothingness' I regard it as the All-Being. Everywhere I have spoken of the Unknowable as the Ultimate Reality—the sole Existence: all things present to consciousness being but shows of it. . . . I might enlarge on the fact that, though the name Agnosticism fitly expresses the confessed inability to know or to conceive the nature of the Power manifested through phenomena, it fails to indicate the confessed ability to recognize the existence of that Power as of all things the most certain. I might make clear the contrast between the Comtean Agnosticism which says that ' Theology and Ontology alike end in the Everlasting No.' . . . with the Agnosticism set forth in [my] ' First Principles of Philosophy,' which . . . emphatically utters an Everlasting Yes. . . . And I might show the error of implying that Agnosticism as I hold it, is any thing more than silent with respect to the question of personality . . . in the conviction that the choice is not between personality and something lower than personality, but between personality and something higher. . . . It is true that we are totally unable to conceive any such higher mode of being . . . But this is not a reason for questioning its existence ; it is rather the reverse. . . . In all imaginable ways we find thrust upon us the truth, that we are not permitted to know—nay, are not permitted even to conceive—that Reality which is behind the veil of Appearance."—(Herbert Spencer.)

Martin Luther's Doctrine of the Unknowable God and the Knowable Logos :

"Although God is omnipresent, He is nowhere ; I cannot lay hold of Him by my own thoughts without the Word. But where He Himself has ordained to be present, there He is certainly to be found. The Jews found Him in Jerusalem at the throne of grace ; we find Him in the Word, in Baptism, in the Lord's Supper. Greeks and Heathens imitated this by building temples for their gods in particular places, in order that they might be able to find them there ; in Ephesus, for example, a temple was built to Diana ; in Delphi to Apollo. *God cannot be found in His Majesty—that is, outside of His revelation of Himself in His Word. The Majesty of God is too exalted and grand for us to be able to grasp it.* He therefore shows us the right way, to wit, Christ, and says, Believe in Him and you will find out who I am, and what are my nature and will. This world meanwhile seeks in innumerable ways with great industry, cost, trouble, and labor, to find the invisible and incomprehensible God in His Majesty. But God is and remains to them unknown, although they have many thoughts about Him, and discourse and dispute much ; *for God has decreed that He will be Unknowable and Unapprehensible apart from Christ.*"—(" Luther's Table Talk.")

That the physical evolution of man has been enormous within the period covered by authentic history, is well-known. When, however, we come to compare the doctrine of the Unknowable, on the one hand, as expressed by Luther, and on the other, as formulated by Herbert Spencer, with the Kabbala, with its doctrine of Divine emanations, derived, we are assured, from the teachings of Zoroaster, it does not seem that the spiritual perceptions of man have made a corresponding advance ; indeed it hardly can be claimed they have held their own ! A comparison of Spencer's doctrine with that of the

Kabbala, goes far to support the view of Laurence Oliphant in his " Scientific Religion," that the Fall of Man coincided with his spirit's assuming a gross animal covering, while the history of human evolution has been the history of the effort of human spirit to raise this vile body into something more worthy to serve as the temple of the Holy Spirit. Says Mathers, in his Introduction to the Kabbala :

" The primal forms of the Unknowable and Nameless One, whom in the more manifest form we speak of as God, are these :

1. Shut Out from Mortal Comprehension.
(a) Ain.
Negative Existence.

(In a seed, the tree which may spring from it is hidden : it is in condition of potential existence ; it is there ; but it will not admit of definition. The seeds which that potential tree may yield are in a condition analogous to potential existence, but are hardly so far advanced. They are *negatively existent.*)

(b) Ain Soph.
Limitless Expanse.
2. Only a Dim Conception Formable :
(c) Ain Soph Aur.
The Illimitable Light.

These three kabbalistic veils of the Negative Existence, viz., Ain—Negativity ; Ain Soph—the Limitless ; and Ain Soph Aur—the Limitless Light, shadow forth to the mind the idea of the Illimitable One. And before that idea, and of that idea, we can only say in the words of an ancient oracle : " In Him is an illimitable abyss of glory, and from it goeth forth one little spark which maketh all the glory of the sun, and of the moon, and of the stars. Mortal ! Behold how little I know of God ; seek not to know more of Him, for this is far beyond thy comprehension, however wise thou art ; as for us who are His ministers, how small a part are we of Him."

This primal Negative Existence, which bears, hidden in itself, positive life, and in the limitless depths of whose negativity lies hidden the power of standing forth from itself, the power of projecting the scintilla of thought into the utter, the power of re-involving the syntagma into the inner ; and which, shrouded and veiled, is the absorbed intensity in the centreless whirl of expansion, manifests in itself ten Sephiroth or Numerical Emanations, of which Number One is Kether, the Crown, and first Sephira. The Divine name attributed to Kether is the name of the Father, given in Exodus iii., 4 : Eheih, I AM. It signifies Existence. Among the epithets applied to Kether, the Crown, are : the Concealed of the Concealed ; the Ancient of the Ancient

6

Ones ; the Most Holy Ancient One ; the Ancient of Days ; the Primordial Point ; the Inscrutable Height.

Among these Sephiroth, jointly and severally, we find the development of the persons and attributes of God. Of these some are male, and some are female. The translators of the Bible have translated a feminine plural by a masculine singular in the case of the word Elohim, thus crowding out of existence the fact that the Deity is both masculine and feminine. Genesis i., 27: " And Elohim prepareth the man in His image ; and in the image of Elohim He prepared him, a male and a female."

" *Eheih, Existence, is the Ancient One.* Macroprospus, the first Sephira, the Crown of the Kabbalistic greatest Trinity, is the *Father in the Christian acceptation of the Trinity.*

" Jehovah contains all the Sephiroth with the exception of Kether, the Crown, and specially signifies Microscopus, and is the *Son in his human incarnation and in the Christian acceptation of the Trinity.*

" The first Sephira, Eheih, the *Crown* (and Father), is called Inscrutable Height ; the remaining Sephiroth, included in *Jehovah* (the Son), are called, respectively, Wisdom, Intelligence, Love, Justice, Beauty, Firmness, Splendour, and Righteousness."

(In comparing Spencer's " Unknowable " with Kabbalism, we must not forget his famous formula of Evolution : " Evolution is an integration of matter and concomitant dissipation of motion ; during which matter *passes from an indefinite, incoherent homogeneity, to a definite, coherent heterogeneity.*")

Between Luther and the Kabbala, stands Swedenborg, who teaches that " Jehovah God Himself descended and became MAN, and became also the Redeemer " ; in support of which doctrine he cites numerous passages of Scripture, such as these :

" Understand that I am He, before Me there was no God formed, and after Me there is none, I—I am Jehovah, and besides Me there is no saviour." —(Isaiah xliii., 10, 11.)

" Thus said Jehovah, King of Israel, and his Redeemer, Jehovah of Hosts ; I am the first and I am the last, and besides Me there is no God."— (Isaiah xliv., 6.)

" I John . . . was in the Spirit on the Lord's-Day, and I heard behind me a great voice, as of a trumpet, saying, ' I am the Alpha and the Omega, the First and the Last ' ; . . . and I did turn to see the voice that did speak to me, and having turned, I saw seven golden lampstands, and in the midst . . . like to a son of man . . . and His countenance as the sun shining in its might. And when I saw Him, I did fall at His feet as dead, and He placed His right hand upon me, saying . . . ' Be not afraid ; I am the First and the Last, and He who is living, and I did become dead, and lo, I am living to the ages of the ages, Amen ! and I have the keys of the hades and of the death.' "—(Rev. i., 9-18.)

(Swedenborg, " The True Christian Religion," n. 82, 83, 102.)

NOTE XII.—"*Music, which is the living God in our bosoms.*"—(P. 32.)

" I well know that God is nearer to me in my art than to others. I communicate with Him without fear ; evermore have I acknowledged and understood Him."—Beethoven.

NOTE XIII.—"*The musical seer, speaking the highest wisdom in a language which Reason does not comprehend, reveals to us the inexpressible truth ; while we listen, we have a presentiment, nay we feel and see that this seemingly substantial world is only a fleeting show.*"—(P. 34.)

" Those vague feelings of unexperienced felicity which music arouses— those indefinite impressions of an unknown ideal life which it calls up, may be considered as a prophecy, to the fulfilment of which music is itself partly instrumental. The strange capacity which we have for being so affected by melody and harmony, may be taken to imply both that it is within the possibilities of our nature to realize those intenser delights they dimly suggest, and that they are in some way concerned in the realization of them. On this supposition the power and the meaning of music become comprehensible ; but otherwise they are a mystery."—(Herbert Spencer, " The Origin and Function of Music.")

NOTE XIV.—"*Our most precious Gospels.*"—(P. 35.)

" In this picture of Jesus we are still happily in the morning light—the dew is on the grass, the mist is in the valley, and a golden radiance from the eastern sky suffuses the Divine form of the Son of Man.

" He walks with his disciples among the Galilean hills, with the red lilies breaking about His feet.

" His Father's voice seems to roll on the summer thunder, the wind that 'bloweth where it listeth' is full of whispers of the heavenly realm, Moses and Elias stand with Him on the shining mount, a strong angel descends to comfort Him in Gethsemane.

" The eye of faith sees Him after the crucifixion in the cool of the day at Emmaus, the hand of doubt touches the nail-prints, the heart of love is quick to discern Him in the dim morning by the quiet lake. In that ineffable Presence no one felt any misgivings—all found rest. The disciples see and believe, the Lord raises His hands in blessing. He is suddenly parted from them, and a bright cloud receives Him out of their sight !

" No time seems able to blur that Vision Beautiful, no skepticism can wither its attractive power. After nineteen centuries of assault and misrepresentation, we can still look on the picture of Jesus, as it stands out in the Gospel Story, and adore without idolatry ; for ' the Word was made flesh and dwelt among us, and we beheld His glory, the glory as of the Only-begotten of the Father, full of Grace and Truth.' "—(" The Picture of Jesus " : Rev. H. A. Haweis, M.A.)

NOTE XV.—" *His Father's voice seems to roll on the summer thunder, the wind that ' bloweth where it listeth' is full of whispers of the heavenly realm.*" —(P. 83.)

" By the immediate consciousness of ourselves alone are we rendered capable of understanding the inner essential nature of things external to ourselves, and that too in such a way that we recognize in them the same fundamental nature which manifests itself in our consciousness of ourselves as being our own. All illusion with regard to this proceeds solely from our seeing a world external to us, which, in the semblance of light, we perceive as something entirely different from us. Our consciousness may at last feel impelled to exclaim with Faust: ' What a spectacle ! But, alas, only a spectacle ! Where can I grasp Thee, Infinite Nature ?' The most certain of answers to this cry is given by music. The outer world speaks to us with such incomparable intelligibility here because by virtue of the effect of sounds, it communicates to us through hearing precisely what we call out to it from the depths of our soul. We understand immediately the cry for help, or of mourning or joy, which we hear, and answer at once in the corresponding sense ; and no illusion, as in the semblance of light, to the effect that the fundamental nature of the world external to us is not completely identical with our own essential nature is possible here ; by which, the gulf that to the sight seems to exist at once vanishes. So the child awakes from the night of the mother's womb with a cry of longing, and the soothing caresses of the mother reply ; so does the longing youth understand the alluring songs of forest birds ; so speaks the moan of animals, the sighing of winds, and the raging shriek of the hurricane to the meditative man who falls into that state of revery in which he perceives through the hearing, that with reference to which his sight has kept him in the illusion of disper[sion] ; *i. e.*, that his inmost nature is one with the inmost nature of all that he perceives, and that only in this perception is the nature of things external to him really recognized."—(Wagner : " Beethoven," pp. 25-7, 33, Schirmer, N. Y.).

" For we have known that all the creation doth groan together, and travail in pain together till now."—(Romans viii., 22.)

Parsifal.—" Methinks to-day the meads are wondrous fair !—
The frondage, flowers, and blossoms,—

> Their fragrance pure as child's delight,
> And speaking fondest trust to me."
>
> *Gurnemanz.*—"'T is all Good Friday's Magic, Lord!"

> *Parsifal.*—" Alas! HIS day of agony!
> When surely all that buds and blooms
> And breathing lives, and lives again,
> Should mourn and weep and sorrow."
>
> —(PARSIFAL, Act III.)

NOTE XVI.—" *To believe in Him is to imitate Him, and to seek union with Him.*"—(P. 36.)

" Prayer in a particular degree pertains to worthy men, because it conjoins them with divinity ; *for similars love to be united together;* but a worthy man is in an eminent degree similar to the divine nature. . . . All nations who have flourished in the exercise of wisdom have applied themselves to divine prayers. . . . Since we are a part of this universe, it is consonant to reason that we should be dependent upon it for support. For a *conversion to the universe* procures safety to everything which it contains. If therefore you possess virtue, it is requisite you should invoke that divinity which previously comprehended . . . every virtue ; for universal good is the cause of that good which belongs to you by participation. And if you seek after some corporeal good, the world is endued with a power which contains universal body. From hence therefore it is necessary that perfection should extend to the parts. We must not conceive (say the ancients) that our prayers cause any animadversion in God, or draw down his beneficence, but rather they are the means of elevating the soul to divinity, and disposing it for the reception of the supernal illumination."—(Porphyry, Neo-Platonist, A.D. 233–305.)

" If we are saved by the love of Christ, it is by love also that we manifest Christ to others. If we have received freely, we also give freely, shining in the midst of night, that is, in the darkness of the world. For so long as this darkness prevails over the earth, Love hangs on the Cross ; because the darkness is the working of a will at variance with the Divine Will, doing continual violence to the Law of Love."—(Dr. A. Kingsford.)

> " Though Christ a thousand times in Bethlehem be born,
> But not within thyself, thy soul will be forlorn :
> The cross of Golgotha thou lookest to in vain,
> Unless within thyself it be set up again."
>
> —(Scheffler, 17th century.)

Note XVII.—"*So the true saint knows that neither by theorizing, disputation, nor controversy can he communicate to the world his inner, deeply blissful intuitions.*"—(P. 36.)

"Words, words,—nay, finally, mere letters and letters, but no living faith !"—(Wagner, 1879, p. 132.)

"The master of the house formerly read to his family and his guests from the costly written book ; now, however, every one reads for himself in silence in printed books, and the author writes for [popularity with] the reader. We must recall the religious sects of the Reformation, with their disputations and petty tracts, in order to gain an insight into the raging delirium that has usurped control over human heads literally 'possessed' with printers' type. It may be assumed that only Luther's glorious choral rescued the healthy spirit of the Reformation, because it stayed the mind and thus healed the cerebral typomania."—Wagner : "Beethoven," p. 4.)

Note XVIII.—"*The only element of Revelation which the world at large can grasp, is dogma.*"—(P. 37.)

A distinction is sometimes drawn between Dogma and Doctrine, as in the following citation :

"Dogmatic Christianity I have allowed to creep into these studies almost as little as it does into the Gospels. The want of definition which Paul, the disciple, already begins to feel, does not seem to have troubled the Master, or, indeed, his followers, during His lifetime. Definitions—explanations suitable to the times, intelligible to the catechumens—naturally enough came later, and no one need object to definitions in creeds or articles which aim at embodying sound and teachable truth for a time—for that is *doctrine.* Every one has a right to object to the definitions of truth framed in one age being riveted *without apology or explanation* upon another—for so *doctrine* is petrified into *dogma.* Most of the schisms and nicknames and heresies and theological miseries in Christendom, much that has sinned against the Life and denied the Gospel of Christ, has come from man's wrong-headed passion for having a fixed definition. . . ."—("The Picture of Jesus," Rev. H. A. Haweis, M.A.)

The position of the "Father of the Pilgrim Fathers," John Robinson, on the question of Doctrine versus Dogma, is manifest from his "counsell to that part of the church of which he was pastor, at their departure from him to begin the great work of Plantation in New England," on which occasion "hee used these expressions . . .":

"We are now ere long to part assunder, and the Lord knoweth whether ever he should live to see our faces again : but whether the Lord had appointed it or not, he charged us before God and his blessed angels, to *follow him no further than he followed Christ. And if God should reveal anything to us by any other instrument of his, to be as ready to receive it, as ever we were to receive any truth by his Ministry : For he was very confident the Lord had more truth and light yet to breake forth out of his holy Word.* He took occasion also miserably to bewaile the state and condition of the Reformed churches, who *were come to a period* in Religion, and *would goe no further than the instruments of their Reformation :* as for example, *the Lutherans, they could not be drawne to goe beyond what Luther saw,* for whatever part of God's will he had further imparted and revealed to Calvin, they will rather die than embrace it. And so also, saith he, you see *the Calvinists, they stick where he left them : A misery much to bee lamented ;* for though they were precious shining lights in their times, yet *God had not revealed his whole will to them :* And were they now living, saith hee, *they would bee as ready and willing to embrace further light, as that they had* received. Here also hee put us in mind of our Church-Covenant whereby wee promise and covenant with God and with one another, *to receive whatsoever light and truth shall bee made known to us from his written Word :* but withal exhorted us to *take heed what wee received for truth, and well to examine and compare, and weigh it with other Scriptures of truth before wee received it ;* for saith hee, *It is not possible the Christian world should come so lately out of such thick Anti-christian darknesse, and that full perfection of knowledge should breake forth at once."*

NOTE XIX.—" *In Christian Love, Faith and Hope are of themselves included."*—(P. 40.)

" Faith and Hope there may and must be, but Love is still the greatest, because it includes the other two, for if we love we must have some Faith in those whom we love, and if we have Faith who shall deprive us of Hope, since in Faith we realise the very substance of things hoped for—the evidence of things not seen. Therefore of Faith, Hope and Love, the greatest of these is Love. It is not a Conception, or a Sentiment, or a Dream, or an Impulse, or an Aspiration. Love is A Way. It is the way out of every difficulty—it is the solvent of every doubt—it brings man close to man—it leads man straight to God through Christ. Love is enough—it takes the place of bodily comfort—it compensates for material losses—it soothes all disappointments—it supplies all needs—it slays death—it is a forctaste of heaven. Paul found it sufficient, and he preached it without the least concealment or misgiving as the one divine panacea for all the ills that could happen to the body or assault and hurt the soul.

" Love meant to St. Paul the self-life merged in the lives of others, yet without the loss of an ever energetic individuality, by which it enriched and built up others with innumerable sympathetic ministries and was itself reciprocally blessed.

" The ground of this love was a Common Humanity. This again had its source in the Central Humanity of God Himself, and thus every true and love-redeemed life was said to be 'hid with Christ in God.' God's human nature remained the ground of our human nature—the central power of that nature was LOVE, or the going forth of Being blessing and to bless. The whole creation was nothing but that—all disorders which had crept into that creation would be set right by that. Human love is delegated power. We who are his offspring have received the spirit of sons and are called upon to love one another, even as He has loved us and given Himself for us.

"The philosophy of this is deep—it will bear inspection on every side. You can put in your test rod anywhere and the living waters will rise.

"In human society that which alone resists disintegration is LOVE.

"The cementing power of the state is not the sword, but self-devotion. You call it patriotism, or allegiance to the throne or the Republic, or enthusiasm for leaders—Paul called it LOVE.

"That which holds families together, and makes people to be of one mind in a house is not interest, or argument, or law, or force, or avarice, or ambition, or selfish pleasure—but LOVE.

"That which tempers the administration of justice is again mercy, or a form of LOVE.

"That which goes forth to seek and to save the lost in our great cities, which feeds the hungry, clothes the naked, which gives to the suffering the necessaries of life, which binds up the broken-hearted, warms the spiritually frost-bound back to life, converts an outward Hell into an inward Paradise, composes discords and brings back peace to a tormented world, making Heaven possible to the soul—is ever LOVE."—("The Picture of Paul": Rev. H. A. Haweis, M.A.)

NOTE XX.—"*This being is also human like myself.*"—(P. 44.)

"Only by means of the highest power of love do we attain true freedom, for there is no true freedom save that which is shared in common by all men, high and low, rich and poor. Two hundred millions of human beings ruthlessly thrown together in the Roman empire, soon found that where all all are not equally free and happy, all must be slaves and miserable."—(Wagner.)

"My friends, if you would see men again the wild beasts they seemed in the nineteenth century, all you have to do is to restore their natural prey in their fellow-men, and to find their gain in the loss of others. No doubt it seems to you that no necessity, however dire, would have tempted you to subsist on what superior skill or strength enabled you to wrest from others equally needy. But suppose it were not merely your own life that you were responsible for. The gentlest creatures are fierce when they have young to provide for. For the sake of those dependent upon him a man might not choose, but must plunge into the foul fight,—cheat, overreach, supplant, defraud, buy below worth and sell above, break down the business by which his neighbor fed his young ones, tempt men to buy what they ought not and sell what they should not, grind his laborers, sweat his debtors, cozen his creditors. Even the ministers of religion were not exempt from this cruel necessity. While they warned their flocks against the love of money, regard for their families compelled them to keep an outlook for the pecuniary prizes of their calling. Poor fellows, theirs was indeed a trying business, preaching to men a generosity and an unselfishness which they and everybody knew would, in the existing state of the world, reduce to poverty those who should practice them; laying down laws of conduct which the law of self-preservation compelled men to break. It is not hard to understand the desperation with which men and women, who under other conditions would have been full of gentleness and truth, fought and tore each other in the scramble for gold, when we realize what it meant to miss it, what poverty was in that day. For the body it was hunger and thirst, torment by heat and frost; in sickness, neglect; in health, unremitting toil; for the moral nature it meant oppression, contempt, and the patient endurance of indignity, brutish associations from infancy, the loss of all the innocence of childhood, the grace of womanhood, the dignity of manhood; for the mind it meant the death of ignorance, the torpor of all those faculties which distinguish us from brutes, the reduction of life to a round of bodily functions. Ah, if such a fate were offered you and your children as the only alternative of success in the accumulation of wealth, how long do you fancy would you be in sinking to the moral level of your ancestors? A number of English prisoners were shut up in a room containing not enough air to supply one tenth of their number. The unfortunates were gallant men, devoted comrades in service, but as the agonies of suffocation began to take hold of them, they forgot all else, and became involved in a hideous struggle, each one for himself, and against all others to force a way to one of the small apertures of the prison at which alone it was possible to get a breath of air. Yet in the Black Hole of Calcutta there were no tender women, no little children and old men and women, no cripples. They were at least all men, strong to bear, who suffered.

"You know the story of that last, greatest, and most bloodless of revolutions. In the time of one generation men laid aside the social traditions and practice of barbarians, and assumed a social order worthy of rational and human beings. Ceasing to be predatory in their habits, they became co-workers, and found in fraternity at once the science of wealth and happiness. 'What shall I eat and drink, and wherewithal shall I be clothed?' stated as a problem beginning and ending in self, had been an anxious and endless one. But when it was conceived not from the individual, but from the fraternal standpoint, 'What shall we eat and drink, and wherewithal shall we be clothed?' its difficulties vanished."—("Looking Backward," by Bellamy.)

NOTE XXI.—"*In all surrounding Nature we see manifested around us the enormous tragedy of earthly existence.*"—(P. 52.)

The foregoing paragraph has a pessimistic sound. Yet Wagner was no absolute pessimist. He anticipated a future state of mankind which, far from being a hateful chaos, should be extremely well ordered, and one in which Religion and Art should not only be preserved, but should, for the first time, attain their true proportions. (Wagner, 1880, p. 294.) As he found in Schopenhauer's philosophy the only adequate foundation for a philosophy of music, without, however, following Schopenhauer in his conclusions that music was the most sinfully sensuous of arts, and the voluptuous Rossini the truest type of musician ; so too Wagner found in Schopenhauer's philosophy, wisely used, the surest, nay, almost the only, way to attain to a rational understanding of the problem of life, without, however, following him in his universal pessimism. Says Wagner : "The assumption of a degeneration of the human race (fall of man), contradictory as it seems to the idea of a steady progress, must be, seriously considered, the only thing which can lead us to a well-grounded hope. The so-called pessimistic view of the world accordingly appears tenable only with the proviso that it is based on the criticism of *historic* man. Pessimism, however, would have to be considerably modified if prehistoric man were to become so far known to us that, from an accurate knowledge of his natural endowments, we could conclude upon a subsequent degeneration which was not unconditionally involved in those natural endowments." (Wagner, 1880, p. 287.) "From the continually ill-advised creations of statesmen we are able to demonstrate most distinctly the bad results of the want of such a knowledge of real human nature. Even Marcus Aurelius could only arrive at a perception of the vanity of the world, without, however, attaining even to the mere assumption of a Fall of a world which perhaps might have been different from the present one, to say nothing of the cause of that fall.* Yet upon

* "It is curious that (materialistic) evolutionism has its fall, like theism ; for if the spiritual nature was awakened by some access of fear, or some grand and terrible physical phenomenon ; and if thus the idea of a higher intelligence was struck out and the descendant of apes became a superstitious and idolatrous savage : that awakening of the religious sense must be so designated. How much trouble and discussion would have been saved had he been aware of his humble origin, and never entertained the vain imagination that he was a child of God, rather than a mere product of physical evolution ! On that theory the awakening of the religious sense and the knowledge of good and evil must surely be designated as a fall of man, since it subverted in his case the previous regular operation of natural selection, and introduced all that debasing superstition, priestly domination, and religious controversy which have been among the chief curses of our race, and which are doubly accursed if, as the evolutionist believes, they are not the ruins of something nobler

the vanity of the world has been based from time immemorial the absolutely pessimistic view, a view by which, merely for the sake of convenience, despotic statesmen and rulers in general willingly suffer themselves to be led." —(Wagner, 1880, p. 333–334.)

" The assumption of our geologists seems to be incontrovertible, that the human race, the last to appear among the animal population of the earth, must have survived a mighty transformation of at least the greater portion of our planet. It is important to form some idea of the changes among the races both of man and animals, which had heretofore multiplied in their primeval native lands, that must necessarily have occurred in consequence of the scattering of all the dwellers upon earth. Certainly the appearance of enormous deserts such as the African Sahara must have driven the dwellers by what had heretofore been luxuriant borderlands surrounding inland seas, into a starvation the terrors of which we can form some idea when we are told of the maddening sufferings of shipwrecked men, by which completely civilized fellow-citizens in modern times have been driven to cannibalism. In the moist river regions of the Canadian lakes, animals allied to the panther and tiger still live as fruit-eaters, while on the borders of the deserts aforesaid the historic lion and tiger have become the most bloodthirsty of beasts. Accordingly, quite abnormal causes are to be assumed by which, in the North American steppes, for instance, among the Malay tribes, hunger has created a thirst for blood."—(Wagner, 1880, p. 288–289.)

" Among the various attempts to recover the lost Paradise, we find in our day associations of the so-called vegetarians ; but precisely there, where attention seems to be fixed upon the very root of the question of Regeneration, we hear from isolated exemplary members the complaint that their comrades, for the most part, abstain from animal food only from personal dietary considerations * ; but in no wise connect with the practice the great and holier, but the mere gratuitous, vain, and useless imaginings of a creature who should have been content to eat and drink and die, without hope or fear, like the brutes from which he sprang."—(Sir John Dawson : " The Story of the Earth and Man.")

" The Tlascalans said that the men who escaped in the Deluge were transformed into apes, but that by degrees they recovered the use of reason and speech." (F. Schultze : " Fetichism.")

* " And God saith, ' Lo, I have given to you every herb sowing seed, which is upon the face of all the earth, and every tree in which is the fruit of a tree sowing seed, to you it is for food ; and to every beast of the earth, and to every fowl of the heavens, and to every creeping thing on the earth, in which is breath of life, every green herb is for food.' "— (Genesis i., 29-30.)

" Eating the flesh of animals, considered in itself, is somewhat profane ; for in the most ancient times they never ate the flesh of any beast or bird, but only grain,—especially bread made of wheat— the fruits of trees, vegetables, milk, and such things as are made from them, as butter, etc."--(Swedenborg.)

" In this paradise man found ample supplies of wholesome and nutritious food. It was probably at the confluence of the rivers that flow into the Euphrates at the head of the moral regenerative thoughts upon which alone it depends, whether or not the Associations shall become a power.

" Next to the vegetarians, and with somewhat more extended practical activity already, come the Societies for the Protection of Animals from Cruelty. Under the guidance of the foregoing societies, and, ennobled by them, the tendency of the so-called Temperance Societies would lead to no less important results. (Wagner, 1880, p. 289-290.) In certain American prisons experiments have shown that the worst criminals were changed by a wisely ordered vegetable diet into gentle and responsible men. Whose memory would the members of these Vegetarian and Temperance Societies, together with that for the Prevention of Cruelty to Animals, commemorate, if, after the labors of the day, they always assembled to refresh themselves with bread and wine?"—(Wagner, 1880, p. 292.)

" Do we still await a new religion which shall preserve us from lapsing into subjection to the power of the blindly raging (selfish) Will in Nature? In our daily meal we are taught to commemorate the Redeemer."—(Wagner, 1880, p. 295.)

" The Lord's Supper is the sole saving rite of the Christian Faith. In its observance lies the fulfilment of the entire teaching of the Saviour. The Christian Church, with anxious torments of conscience, perpetuates this teaching without ever being able to bring it into use in its purity; although, seriously considered, that teaching should form the most universally comprehensible kernel of Christianity. The Lord's Supper early became transformed into a symbolic action by priests,* while its true sense continued to be expressed only in the fasts occasionally prescribed, a strict observance of

---

Persian Gulf. . . . Its flora afforded abundance of edible fruits. . . ."—(Sir John Dawson: " The Story of the Earth and Man.")

According to the doctrine of evolution, the present structure of the carnivorous animals does not contradict the statement above quoted from Genesis i., 29-30.

*One of the most interesting of the changes from the original form of the Lord's Supper was the change from the use of simple bread to that of wafers. These wafers carry us back to the Persian sun worship, in the sacrament of which the bread used was a " round cake," *emblem of the solar disk,* and called Mizd. This religion, known as Mithracism, first made its appearance in Italy upon Pompey's reduction of the Cilician pirates. Constantine retained upon his coinage, long after his conversion, the figure of Sol, with the legend: " To the invincible Sun, my Guardian," a type capable of a double interpretation, meaning equally the ancient Phœbus and the new Sun of Righteousness. Similarly the old festival held on the 25th day of December in honor of the Birthday of the Invincible One, and celebrated by the great Games of the Circus, was transferred to the commemoration of the birth of Christ, of which the Fathers say the real day was unknown. In like manner, hot-cross buns remind one of the " Bouns or cakes of flour, oil, and honey of the Egyptians, Assyrians, and Jews (Jeremiah xliv., 18-19), and also of the round cakes (the chaputty of evil notoriety at the outbreak of the Sepoy mutiny) which are, among the Hindoos, the established offering to the Manes of their ancestors.—(See " The Gnostics and their Remains," by King.)

it being imposed at last upon certain religious orders only, and even there more in the sense of an act of self-renunciation, promoting humility, than of a physical and spiritual means of salvation. Perhaps the impossibility of insisting that all who professed Christianity should continually follow this ordinance of the Saviour by wholly abstaining from animal food was one of the main causes of the early fall of the Christian religion as a Christian Church."—(Wagner, 1880, pp. 283–284.)

As Wagner gives no authority for his views touching the nature and end of the Lord's Supper, the present writer has consulted the Rev. Dr. Neale's collection of all known forms of institution. Of the eighty-two forms there given, the following one, called Syro-Jacobite, and taken from the first liturgy of St. Peter (the primitive communion office was liturgical ; see "The Teaching of the Twelve Apostles," by Rev. Dr. Schaff), is especially significant :

"And when he was preparing that banquet of His Body and Holy Blood, imparting it to us, and near was His salutary Passion, He took bread in His immaculate Hands, and lifted it up, and vouchsafed to bestow upon it His visible aspect and insensible benediction, and blessed it, and sanctified it, and gave it to the disciples, His Apostles, and said : Let these mysteries be the support of your journey ; *and whenever ye eat this in the way of food*, believe and be certain that this is my Body, which for you and for many is broken and is given for you for the Expiation of Transgressions, the Remission of Sins and Life Eternal. . . . In like manner the Chalice also ; after He had supped, He mingled water and wine, and blessed and sanctified it, and gave to the disciples, His Apostles, saying : Take, drink ye all of it ; for this is my Blood of the New Testament which for you and for many is poured and given for the Pardon of Transgressions, the Remission of Sins, and Eternal Life. . . . And that they might receive the most sweet fruit of that divine operation, He commanded them after this fashion : As often as ye shall be gathered together, keep memory of Me, and eating this offered bread, and drinking this prepared cup, ye shall do it in remembrance of Me and shall confess My death, until I come."—(Dr. Neale.)

. . . .

"The primitive Eucharist embraced the Agape and the Communion proper. . . . The Christian Agape was a much simpler feast than the Jewish Passover. Tertullian describes it as a ' school of virtue rather than a banquet,' and says ' as much is eaten as satisfies the cravings of hunger ; as much is drunk as befits the chaste.' But occasional excesses of intemperance occurred already in Apostolic congregations, as at Corinth, and must have multiplied with the growth of the Church. Early in the second century the social Agape was separated from the Communion, and held in the evening, the more solemn Communion in the morning ; and afterwards the

Agape was abandoned altogether, or changed into a charity for the poor."—
(Schaff : " The Teaching of the Twelve Apostles.")

" He took bread and wine to teach the doctrine of life and sacrifice, of
union with Himself and with each other, and He said, ' This is My Body
and Blood,' just as He said, ' I am the Door—the Shepherd—the Vine.'
Was He a Door, a Shepherd, a Tree ? Was it His Body and Blood? It
was the sign, the symbol, and the outward rite was given as a memorial of
Himself, as a means of realizing spiritually the life imaged in the nourishing
bread ; the sacrifice imaged in the sign of the blood-red wine ; the union
imaged in the common food, uniting the Christian group to Himself and to
one another in the common fellowship of a common meal. . . . In every
Christian household it was usual for the head of the family at the evening
meal to hand round bread and wine ' in remembrance ' of Him. . . . From
a social usage this act at the family supper grew into an ecclesiastical sacrament, administration being only valid after consecration by the priests, and
thus became, in the hands of the Church, a sort of magical rite of mysterious efficacy, to be granted or withheld at the good-will and pleasure of the
clergy. . . . Far may we have travelled from the simplicity which is in
Jesus, but if we wish to know what he meant we must go back and assist at
the first celebration in that upper room after the departure of Judas, and
then all forms will be equally good for us ; or at least tolerated by us. We
shall be free ; we shall see the Lord's intent, simple and pure, through every
mist and veil of man's invention, and we shall use the rite as an intense and
earnest form of prayer, summing up the great cardinal points of Christianity,
Christ's life, Christ's sacrifice, our union with each other, Christ's union with
us and ours with Him."—(" The Picture of Jesus," Rev. II. A. Haweis, M.A.)

NOTE XXII.—" *The human race must have survived a mighty transformation of at least the greater portion of our planet.*"—(P. 91.)*

" Consider the greatness of that Creator . . . by whatever name we
like to call Him, . . . who has in some inscrutable way set all this
stupendous machinery in motion ; yes, and as perfect in its colossal and
illimitable whole, as in its minutest details,—in the path of the sun through
the wastes of space, as in the flash of the lightning along our wires, or in the

* The notes prepared on this point have assumed such proportions that they must
be reserved for a separate work to follow the " Parsifal," entitled, " The Lost Pleiad ;
or, the Fall of Lucifer, the Key to the Solar Myths and the Origin of all Known Forms
of Religion." The conclusion developed by the testimony gathered being, that, in
Christianity, far from "something small and local" (*vide* " Robert Elsmere "), we
possess the religion of Prehistoric Man, and that it is now in process of being re-es-
tablished upon its ancient intellectual foundations largely by the involuntary agency
of Modern Science. The hypothesis is outlined in the above selections ; the
demonstration must be reserved for the book to follow.

structure of the insect's wing. . . . Let us try to realize what all these motions really mean, and what the result of the sudden disarrangement, not to say stoppage, of any one of them in our own system would be . . . the catastrophe would be of so stupendous a nature that we could hardly conjecture its effect."—(Gen. Forlong : " Rivers of Faith.")

" The scientist Bode entertained the opinion that the planetary distances above Mercury formed a geometrical series, . . . but this law seemed to be interrupted between Mars and Jupiter. Hence he inferred that there was a planet wanting in the interval ; which is now supplied by the discovery of the numerous star-form planets occupying the very place of the unexplained vacancy. . . . Many eminent astronomers are of the opinion that these telescopic planets are the fragments of a large celestial body which once revolved between Mars and Jupiter, and which burst asunder by some tremendous convulsion. . . . From this discovery, Dr. Olbers first conceived the idea that these bodies might be the fragments of a former world.* . . . Dr. Brewster attributes the fall of meteoric stones to the smaller fragments of these bodies happening to come within the sphere of the earth's attraction."—(Burritt's " Geography of the Heavens," revised by Mattison, 1873.)

" According to the Kabbalah, there were certain primordial worlds created, but these could not subsist, as the equilibrium of the balance was not yet perfect, and they were convulsed by the unbalanced force and destroyed. These primordial worlds are called (in Scripture) the ' kings of ancient time,' and the ' kings of Edom who reigned between the monarchs of Israel.' "—Genesis xxxvi., 31.—(Mathers : " Kabbalah Unveiled.")

" It is the opinion of many that the planetoids (asteroids) are the fragments of a planet which has been destroyed. The idea has been advanced that this planet was the seat of a fallen race, and that the ' powers and principalities of the air,' against which the people of this earth have to contend, are in reality the lost souls of the planet in question. . . . [Sir W. Thomson and Prof. Helmholtz agree in suggesting the meteoric hypothesis as a possible way of accounting for the origin of terrestrial life, its germs having been wafted to us from some other world or its fragments. See pp. 102-103.] Many supposed mythological traditions of ancient Greece have been shown to have a foundation in history ; and we may assume that this is possibly the case to a far greater extent than has yet been proven, and that it applies to other localities and peoples as well. Isaiah makes reference to

---

* " While recognizing the incompleteness of the evidence, it seems to me to go far to justify the hypothesis of Olbers . . . that the planetoids resulted from the bursting of a planet once revolving in the region they occupy . . . and is quite incongruous with that of Laplace."—(" The Nebular Hypothesis," by Herbert Spencer, originally printed in 1864, revised and extended to present the author's latest views, 1883.)

Lucifer as having falling from his shining place in the heavens, and intimates that its people were not suffered to rest even in their graves (Isaiah, xiv., 12–16, 19). This would be literally true if the planet had been destroyed. We have to confront numerous traditions regarding the fallen race,—tempters of Adam and Eve, etc. The Talmud speaks of the ancient people of earth as having faces that shone like the sun, and natures that reached into the heavens. The ' morning star' has vanished, and where once was unity, light, and power, we now have but a confused mass of planetoids moving in eccentric orbits. The extremity of individualism stands exemplified, and the mind and nature of humanity is broken and divided in like manner, for this was not merely the experience of a planet, but a tragedy of the solar system, the effect of which is spread over thousands of years, though it is probable that we are now well advanced in the restoration of order. . . . Will this lost star be re-lit in the material heavens ? We judge not. The solar system has established a new equilibrium. . . . Was this calamity unforeseen ? We judge not. Man's extremity is said to be God's opportunity ; and from that period dates a new cycle of this solar system. Neither this earth, nor yet the solar system, are complete in themselves, but are merely parts, physically and spiritually, of one perfect whole. . . . In the career of Abraham, Isaac, and Jacob, and the Twelve Tribes of Israel, we see a process of spiritual development culminating in the advent of Christ, in whom the nature of the human race becomes enjoined again to the order of the heavens. . . . There is a law of involution as well as of evolution, and there must be some point where forces meet and balance, or find equilibrium. Humanity ascends (evolution) and unfolds into spirit ; spirit descends (involution) and finds embodiment in humanity. If not a sparrow falls to the ground without notice, it is presumable that the fall of Lucifer is not without an ultimate good to this earth and solar system, and as a necessary consequence to the countless worlds of the starry heavens. Christ stood in the place of the fallen son of the morning. The new heaven was to replace the fallen star. According to His own testimony, He and His Father were one, and all power was given into His hands, both in the heavens and on the earth. This is a vast saying, yet what if it be true ? It is not inconsistent with the mysteries and wonders of the heavens. . . . Nor ought we to deem it inconsistent with the mysteries of the Luminous and Mighty One of the heavens that He should once have walked this earth. . . . thereby joining the least to the greatest, and carrying aloft the chords of this human nature, thereby rendering mortal access easy, and the kingdom of heaven on earth not only possible, but certain."—(John Latham, selected.)

" It is the god incarnate, more than the God of the Jews or of Nature, who . . . has taken so great and salutary a hold on the modern mind. And what ever else may be taken away from us, . . . Christ is still left ; a unique figure, not more unlike all his precursors than all his followers, even those who had the benefit of his personal teaching. It is of no use to say that Christ as exhibited in the Gospels is not historical, and that we know not how much of what is admirable has been superadded by the tradition of his followers. . . . Who among his disciples or among their proselytes was capable of inventing the sayings ascribed to Jesus, or of imagining the life and character revealed in the Gospels ? Certainly not the fishermen of Galilee ; as certainly not St. Paul, whose character and idiosyncrasies were of a totally different sort ; still less the early Christian writers, in whom nothing is more evident than that the good which was in them was all derived, as they always professed that it was derived, from the higher source.

But about the life and sayings of Jesus there is a stamp of personal originality, combined with profundity of insight, which . . . must place the Prophet of Nazareth . . . in the very first rank of the men of sublime genius of which our species can boast, . . . combined with the qualities of probably the greatest moral reformer, and martyr of that mission, who ever existed upon earth. . . . To the conception of the rational sceptic it remains a possibility that Christ actually was . . . charged with a special, express, and unique commission from God to lead mankind to truth and virtue. . . . "—(John Stuart Mill : " Three Essays on Religion.")

" Those who admit my interpretation of the evidence now adduced—strictly scientific evidence in its appeal to facts which are clearly what ought *not* to be, on the materialistic theory—will be able to accept the spiritual nature of man as not in any way inconsistent with the theory of evolution, but as dependent upon those fundamental laws and causes which furnish the very materials for evolution to work with. They will also be relieved from the crushing mental burden imposed upon those who—maintaining that we, in common with the rest of nature, are but products of the blind eternal forces of the universe, and believing also that the time must come when the sun will lose his heat and all life on the earth necessarily cease—have to contemplate a not very distant future in which all this glorious earth—which, for untold millions of years has been slowly developing forms of life and beauty to culminate at last in man—shall be as if it never had existed ; who are compelled to suppose that all the slow growths of our race struggling towards a higher life, all the agony of martyrs, all the groans of victims, all the evil and misery and undeserved suffering of the ages, all the struggles for freedom, all the efforts towards justice, all the aspirations for virtue and the well-being of humanity, shall absolutely vanish, and, ' like the baseless fabric of a vision, leave not a wrack behind.' As contrasted with this hopeless and soul-deadening belief, we who accept the existence of a spiritual world can look upon the universe as a grand, consistent whole, adapted in all its parts to the development of spiritual beings capable of indefinite life

7

and perfectibility.   To us the whole purpose, the only *raison d'être* of the world—with all its complexities of physical structure, with its grand geological progress, the slow evolution of the vegetable and animal kingdoms, and the ultimate appearance of man—was the development of the human spirit in association with the human body.   From the fact that the spirit of man—the man himself—*is* so developed, we may well believe that this is the only, or at least the best, way for its development ; and we may even see, in what is usually termed 'evil' on the earth, one of the most efficient means of its growth.   For we know that the noblest faculties of man are strengthened and perfected by struggle and effort ; it is by unceasing warfare against physical evils and in the midst of difficulty and danger that energy, courage, self-reliance, and industry have become the common qualities of the northern races ; it is by the battle with moral evil in all its hydra-headed forms, that the still nobler qualities of justice and mercy and humanity and self-sacrifice have been steadily increasing in the world.   Beings thus trained and strengthened by their surroundings, and possessing latent faculties capable of such noble development, are surely destined for a higher and more permanent existence. . . .   We thus find that the Darwinian theory, even when carried out to its extreme logical conclusion, not only does not oppose, but lends a decided support to, a belief in the spiritual nature of man.   It shows us how man's body may have been developed from that of a lower animal form under the law of natural selection, but it also teaches us that we possess intellectual and moral faculties which could not have been so developed, but must have had another origin ; and for this origin we can find an adequate cause only in the unseen universe of Spirit."—(Alfred Russel Wallace : "Darwinism," 1889.) *

NOTE XXIII.—" *Our existence shows itself beyond our persons, by direct participation in the thoughts of other individuals, and by the power of knowing the absent, the distant, and even the future.   It is a mere illusion that limits our existence to our persons.*"—(P. 54.)

To understand the full force of this illustration, it is necessary to recall the investigations of Schopenhauer's great master and forerunner, Emanuel Kant, the celebrated author of the "Critique of Pure Reason," touching the reality of the "power of knowing the absent, the distant, and even the

---

* "Early in 1856 Lyell advised me to write out my views pretty fully" ("Origin of Species "). " and I began at once to do so. . . . But my plans were overthrown, for, early in the summer of 1858, Mr. Wallace, then in the Malay Archipelago, sent me an essay . . . containing exactly the same theory as mine."—(Darwin : " Autobiography.") " You must let me say how I admire the generous manner in which you speak of my book (' Origin of Species '). Most persons would, in your position, have felt some envy or jealousy. But you speak far too modestly of yourself. You would, if you had my leisure, have done the work just as well—perhaps better than I have done it."—Darwin : " Letter to Alfred Russel Wallace," 1860.)

future." In 1766, Kant published an attack on Swedenborg, entitled "Dreams of a Ghost Seer Illustrated by Dreams of Metaphysics." Two years after, in 1768, having sifted the matters about to be recalled here, to the utmost, by a circle of inquiries, epistolary as well as personal, Kant wrote as follows to Charlotte Von Knobloch, a lady of quality : "On Saturday, at 4 o'clock, P.M., when Swedenborg arrived at Gottenburg from England, Mr. Wm. Castel invited him to his house, together with a party of fifteen persons. About 6 o'clock Swedenborg went out, and after a short interval returned to the company, quite pale and alarmed. He said that a dangerous fire had just broken out in Stockholm, at the Sodermalm (Gottenburg is 300 miles from Stockholm), and that it was spreading very fast. He was restless, and went out often. He said that the house of one of his friends, whom he named, was already in ashes, and that his own was in danger. At 8 o'clock, after he had been out again, he joyfully exclaimed : 'Thank God ! The fire is extinguished the third door from my house.' This news occasioned great commotion throughout the whole city, and particularly amongst the company in which he was. It was announced to the Governor the same evening. On the Sunday morning Swedenborg was sent for by the Governor, who questioned him concerning the disaster. Swedenborg described the fire precisely, how it had begun, in what manner it had ceased, and how long it had continued ; and as the Governor had thought it worthy of attention, the consternation was considerably increased, because many were in trouble on account of their friends and property which might have been involved in the disaster. On the Monday evening a messenger arrived at Gottenburg, who was despatched during the time of the fire. In the letters brought by him the fire was described precisely in the manner stated by Swedenborg. On the Tuesday morning the royal courier arrived at the Governor's with the melancholy intelligence of the fire, of the loss which it had occasioned, and of the houses it had damaged and ruined, not in the least differing from that which Swedenborg had given immediately it had ceased, for the fire was extinguished at 8 o'clock. What," continues Kant, "can be brought forward against the authenticity of this occurrence ? My friend who wrote this to me has not only examined the circumstances of this extraordinary case at Stockholm, but also, about two months ago, at Gottenburg, where he is acquainted with the most respectable houses, and where he could obtain the most authentic and complete information, as the greater part of the inhabitants, who are still alive, were witnesses to the memorable occurrence."

Another instance in the line of Schopenhauer's illustration, also verified by Kant at the time, was that concerning Louisa Ulrica, a sister of Frederick the Great of Prussia, who was married to King Adolphus of Sweden. Queen Louisa received a letter from the Duchess of Brunswick, in which she mentioned that she had read in the Gottingen *Gazette* an account of a man at Stockholm who pretended to speak with the dead. . . . Says Captain Stalhammer (one of the many authorities whose narratives of what passed between Swedenborg and the Queen have been preserved) : "A short time after the death of the Prince of Prussia Swedenborg came to court (being summoned thither by the senator, Count Scheffer). As soon as he was perceived by the Queen she said to him : 'Well, Mr. Assessor, have you seen my brother?' Swedenborg answered : 'No.' Whereupon she replied : 'If you should see him, remember me to him.' Eight days afterward . . . Swedenborg came to court . . . so early that the Queen had not left her apartment called the white room, where she was conversing with her maids of honor and other ladies. Swedenborg did not wait . . . but entered directly into the Queen's apartment and whispered in her ear. The Queen, struck with astonishment, was taken ill, and did not recover herself for some time. After she came to herself she said to those about her : 'There is only God and my brother who can know what he has just told me.' She owned that he had just spoken of her last correspondence with the prince, the subject of which was known to themselves alone." Of Swedenborg the captain adds : "I knew him for many years, and I can confidently affirm that he was as fully persuaded that he conversed with spirits as I am that I am writing at this moment. As a citizen and as a friend he was a man of the greatest integrity, abhorring imposture, and leading an exemplary life."

Says the Chevalier Beylon : "I found an opportunity of speaking with the Queen herself concerning Swedenborg, and she told me the anecdote respecting herself and her brother with a conviction which appeared extraordinary to me. Every one who knew this truly enlightened sister of the great Frederick will give me credit when I say that she was by no means enthusiastic or fanatical, and that her entire mental character was wholly free from such conceits. Nevertheless, she appeared to me to be so convinced of Swedenborg's supernatural intercourse with spirits that I scarcely durst venture to intimate some doubts . . . for when she perceived my suspicion, she said with a royal air : 'I am not easily duped.' And thus she put an end to all my attempts at refutation."—("Emanuel Swedenborg ; a Biographical Sketch," by J. J. G. Wilkinson, M.D.)

"That death is the bourne from which no traveller has ever returned, has always seemed to me a poetic but unwarranted assumption. . . . There was probably never a time in the history of the world when thousands of people, by no means lunatics, were not convinced that the dead were alive ; that they were able by thought, word, or deed to make their existence felt ; that they occasionally had appeared. Such beliefs, founded, it is often said, on imposture or delusion, have been smitten by modern science with paralysis, and are fast dying out amongst educated people ; which reads extremely well, only facts are against the theory, since it would be difficult to point to any past age in which there were so many thousands of educated people as are at present convinced that the dead are alive, that they are able by thought, word, and deed to make their presence felt, and that they have occasionally 'appeared.' . . . A supernatural vein will be found running through all history, sacred and profane. . . . For my part, with the obvious limitation—suggested by the prevalence of imposture, the human liability to err, and the equally human propensity to be deceived—I find it easier to admit the occurrence of some so-called supernatural events in history, sacred and profane, both in times past and present, than to deny it with the superficial, ignore it with the scientific, or explain it away with the sceptical . . . and the explanations which are put forward to get rid of such evidence as there is, have always seemed to me quite as wonderful and not quite as credible as the alleged occurrences which they are intended to get rid of."—("The Picture of Jesus" : Rev. H. A. Haweis, M.A.)

The great scientific principle of the Law of Continuity means that the whole universe is of a piece ; that it is something which an intelligent being is capable of understanding better and better the more he studies it.*

Let us suppose that the sun, moon, and stars were to move about in strange and fantastic orbits during one day, after which they returned to their previous courses. Here we should have an example of a breach of Continuity, for even if things were so arranged as to prevent physical disaster, it is evident that the whole intelligent universe would be plunged into irretrievable mental confusion. Never again would it be said that Astronomy is competent to explain the varied motions of the heavenly bodies.† But the concluding words of the Te Deum have been abundantly fulfilled in the experience of the astronomer. He has trusted in God, and he has never been confounded.‡

Continuity does not preclude the occurrence of strange, abrupt, unforeseen events in the universe, but only of such events as must finally and forever put to confusion the intelligent beings who regard them.§

Now we can hardly escape from the conclusion that the visible universe must come to an end. But the principle of Continuity still demanding a continuance of the universe, we are forced to believe that there is something beyond that which is visible,—that "the things which are seen are temporal, but the things which are not seen are eternal." ‖

* " The Unseen Universe," § 264.
† " The Unseen Universe," § 76.
‡ " The Unseen Universe," § 74.
§ " The Unseen Universe," § 76.
‖ " The Unseen Universe," § 84.

Again, it is perfectly certain that the visible universe must have had a beginning in time ; but if it be all that exists, then the first abrupt manifestation of it is as truly a break of Continuity as its final overthrow.*

In fine, the visible universe cannot comprehend the whole works of God, because it had its beginning in time, and will also come to an end. Perhaps it forms only an infinitesimal portion of that stupendous whole which is alone entitled to be called The Universe.†

We are led by scientific logic to an unseen, and by scientific analogy to the spirituality of this unseen ; in fine, that the visible universe has been developed by an intelligent resident in the Unseen.‡

Life can be produced from life only. It is some time since science gave up the idea that life could generate energy ; it now seems that we must give up the idea that energy can generate life.§

In both worlds, alike of energy and of life, the principle of Continuity requires that, to account for the origin of phenomena, we shall not resort to the hypothesis of separate creations. Darwin especially imagines that all the present organisms, including man, may have been derived by the process of natural selection from a single primordial germ. When, however, the backward process has reached this germ, an insuperable difficulty presents itself. How was this germ produced ? All scientific experience tells us that life can be produced from a living antecedent only ; what then was the antecedent of this germ ? We are thus forced to contemplate an antecedent possessing life and giving life to this primordial germ, an antecedent in the universe. Life is always produced from life, but like is by no means always produced from like. In this case, more especially, the living antecedent must be in the invisible universe, and therefore altogether different from the visible germ.‖

Our hypothesis, in which the material as well as the life of the visible universe are regarded as having been developed from the Unseen, in which they had existed from Eternity, presents the only available method of avoiding a break of Continuity, if we are to accept loyally the indications given by observation and experiment. It thus appears, . . . that the visible universe is *not* eternal, and that it has *not* the power of originating life. Life as well as matter comes to us from the Unseen Universe.¶

The explanation of the origin of life proposed by Sir W. Thomson had also occurred to Professor Helmholtz. This latter physicist, in an article on the use and abuse of the deductive method in Physical Science (*Nature*

---

* "The Unseen Universe," § 85.
† "The Unseen Universe," § 86.
‡ "The Unseen Universe," § 221.
§ "The Unseen Universe," § 229.
‖ "The Unseen Universe," § 230.
¶ "The Unseen Universe," § 243.

January 14, 1875), tells us very clearly what led himself, and no doubt Sir W. Thomson likewise, to suggest the meteoric hypothesis as a possible way of accounting for the origin of terrestrial life: "If failure attends all our efforts to obtain a generation of organisms from lifeless matter, it seems to me [says Professor Helmholtz] a thoroughly correct procedure to inquire whether it is not as old as matter, and whether its germs, borne from one world to another, have not been developed wherever they have found a favorable soil."

Thus, according to the meteoric hypothesis, germs may have been wafted to us from some other world or its fragments, and thus one act of creation might possibly serve for many worlds.*

Two great laws come before us, the one of which is the Conservation of Mass and of Energy, pointing, as the most probable solution, to an intelligent Agent, one of whose functions it is to develop the universe objectively considered; while the other law is that of Biogenesis, in virtue of which the appearance of a living being in the universe denotes the existence of an antecedent possessing life, thus leading to the conclusion that there is an intelligent Agent, one of whose functions it is to develop intelligence and life. But these conclusions, which most simply and naturally satisfy the principle of Continuity, so far as they go appear to agree with the Christian doctrine.†

There is a record which claims to give us the history of a communication with the spiritual intelligences of the unseen. If it is true it must teach us many things which science is utterly incompetent to reveal. But science alone gives us, by logic and analogy combined, a certain insight into this interesting and mysterious region. Working our way upwards, we have reached, by the principle of Continuity, certain regions. Working their way downward, the Christian records have reached these same regions of thought.‡ Not only are the nebulous beginning and fiery termination of the present visible universe indicated by the Christian records, but a constitution and a power are therein assigned to the Unseen Universe strikingly analogous to those at which we arrive by a legitimate scientific process. Thus the result of questioning science without mistrust or hesitation, under the guidance of legitimate principles, is that science, instead of appearing antagonistic to the claims of Christianity, is in reality its most efficient supporter; and the burden of showing how the early Christains got hold of a constitution of the unseen universe altogether different from any other cosmogony, but similar to that which modern science proclaims, rests upon the shoulders of the opponents of Christianity.

* "The Unseen Universe." §§ 238-9.
† "The Unseen Universe," § 244.
‡ "The Unseen Universe," § 221.

The truth is, that science and religion neither are nor can be two fields of knowledge with no possible communication between them. There is an avenue leading from the one to the other through the unseen universe, but unfortunately it has been walled up and ticketed with "no road this way," professedly alike in the name of Science at the one end and in the name of Religion at the other.

Whether we take the scientific or the religious point of view, one great object of our life in the visible universe is obviously to learn, and advance in learning implies a high purpose kept steadily before us, and an arduous pursuit. "This is the victory which overcometh the world, even our faith." *

"Through faith we understand that the worlds were framed by the word of God ; so that things which are seen were not made of things which do appear."—(Hebrews xi., 3.)

"Faith is belief in the unknown portion of the grand totality, whose existence is demonstrated by its known parts ; it can be no negation of reason, and the object of faith being necessarily hypothetical in form, since knowledge, not faith, alone can define, all definitions of it are a confusion of faith and science. The true act of faith, therefore, consists solely in the adhesion of our intelligence to the immovable and universal reason, which excludes all monstrosity and falsehood from the domain of first causes. The Reasonable Being supposes necessarily the *raison d'etre*, it is the absolute, it is the law. God himself, in whatever manner he conceived, cannot exist without *raison d'etre*, only insanity will provide a personal, arbitrary, and inexplicable authority as the cause of immutable law. The impossible, unmerited, and irresponsible supremacy of God would be the highest of injustices, and the most revolting of absurdities. What, then, is Deity for us ? It is the undefined conception of a *Supreme Personality*. . . . True certitude is the reciprocal acquiescence of the reason which knows in the sentiment which believes, and of the sentiment which believes in the reason which knows."—("The Mysteries of Magic" : A. E. Waite.)

"The effort of the human intellect is to explain the world and man. Trusting the illusion of the senses, the ancient Greeks set astronomy the task of explaining the apparent movements of the sun, planets, and fixed stars, on the supposition that they were the true ones. But the thought of Copernicus—anticipated in the secret teaching of Pythagoras and the Kabbalah—exposed the sense-illusion in which human understanding lay imprisoned. Philosophy would explain the world. But what world ? The world manifested to us by our senses. And philosophy, like astronomy, took the appearance for the reality. It was believed that the whole real world, as it lay outside of us, projected itself, by means of our sense-apparatus, into our brain ! Thus the materialist is imprisoned in appearance, and holds the

---

* "The Unseen Universe," §§ 264-6.

world to be just what it is for his senses. But, says Huxley, in one of his Lay Sermons : ' When materialists talk about there being nothing in the world but matter and force and necessary laws, I decline to follow them. Matter and force are, so far as we can know, mere names for certain forms of consciousness ; meanwhile, as Descartes tells us, "Our knowledge of the soul is more intimate and certain than our knowledge of the body."—Darwin has proved that from the standpoint of organism, a transcendental world is continually given, and Kant has proved the same thing for man by his distinction between the "thing in itself" and the phenomenon. We know now that we cannot grasp the reality with our present number of senses. We thus find ourselves at a masquerade, since we are not truly cognizant of the reality of things, but only of the modes in which our senses react upon them.'

" The result of human thought upon the world-problem may thus be expressed by saying : Consciousness does not exhaust its object, the World.

" We pass to the second great problem for the intellect : Man. As the world is the object of consciousness, so is the Ego the object of self-consciousness. As regards the world and consciousness, the conception of materialism has been eliminated ; but it is still partially maintained in regard to self-consciousness and the Ego. Materialism still flatters itself with the hope of being able to reduce all psychology to physiology. But here again we find that our self-consciousness does not exhaust its object, the Ego, for corresponding to the transcendental world we find a transcendental Ego ; hence our sense of personality, by which we know ourselves, does not coincide with our whole Ego. The sphere of our earthly personality is only the smaller circle included in the larger concentric circle of our metaphysical Subject, and our earthly self-consciousness does not cast its beams to the periphery of our being. Man is a monistic double-being, having two persons, one empirical, the other transcendental. Our normal self-consciousness does not exhaust its object, our Self—it comprehends only one of the two persons of our Subject, namely, the empirical, not the transcendental.

" Somnambulism proves that Schopenhauer and Hartmann are right in laying at the foundation of human phenomena a Will and an Unconscious ; but it also proves that *this Will is not blind*, and that what to the Ego is unconscious, *is not unconscious in itself ;* that between us and the world-substance a transcendental Subject must be interposed, a willing and knowing being ; that thus *the individuality of man avails beyond his temporary phenomenal form, and the earthly existence is only one of the many possible forms of existence of our Subject. . . .* The human psyche, *not by exaltation of sense consciousness, but on suppression of the same, reveals powers which physiologically are quite inexplicable*, hence the soul is something else than the *effect* of the organism, thinking is something else than a mere secretion of the brain. *The substance of man belonging to the transcendental world,* existing behind the sense-consciousness, and only exceptionally encroaching upon it, *is the prime cause of the organism. . . .* It is certain that in man there is a kernel to which the laws of sensibility do not apply—an organ for which the cognitional forms of time and space avail differently than for the sense-consciousness. Since the functions of this organ *attain to freer activity in the degree that the sense-consciousness is suppressed,* so that the latter shows itself to be a hindrance to the development of that activity, it follows that the total annulment of our sense-consciousness can only be looked upon as a total removal of this hindrance ; thus *death does not affect the true substance of man ; nay, it permits the cognitional mode which was suppressed in the earthly life again to attain unimpeded activity. . . .* We possess our past in the form of images lying in our memory. The feeling of personality arises because we refer the succession of our experiences to an identical Subject which knows itself as permanent in all change of the feelings. . . . As the plant grows in the light, but its roots are sunk in the dark bosom of the earth, so is our Ego sunk with a metaphysical root in an order of things lying beyond our knowledge. . . . There is certainly a world beyond, that is, beyond our consciousness ; in other words, our sense-consciousness has its limits just in its senses ; we ourselves belong already now to that world beyond, so far as our Ego exceeds self-consciousness, thus as—but only relatively—unconscious beings. We are not temporarily and spatially divided from that world beyond, are not first transposed there by death, but are already rooted therein, and what divides us therefrom is merely the subjective barrier of our threshold of sensibility. . . . Were our five senses suddenly taken away, and senses of an entirely different kind given to us, though standing on the same spot, we should believe ourselves inhabitants of another star."—(" The Philosophy of Mysticism " : Baron du Prel.)

" If we are abroad in the storm of tempestuous seas, where the mountainous waves rise and fall, dash themselves furiously against steep cliffs, and toss their spray high in the air ; while the storm howls, the sea boils, the lightning flashes from black clouds, and the peals of thunder drown the voice of storm and sea,—then, in the undismayed beholder, the twofold nature of his consciousness reaches the highest degree of distinctness. He perceives himself, on the one hand, as an individual, as the frail phenomenon of will, which the slightest touch of these forces can utterly destroy, helpless against powerful nature, dependent, the victim of chance, a vanishing nothing in the presence of stupendous might ; and, on the other hand, he perceives himself as the eternal, peaceful, knowing subject, the condition of the object, and therefore the supporter of this whole world ; the terrific strife of nature only his idea ; the subject itself free and apart from all desires and necessities, in the quiet comprehension of the Ideas. This is the complete impression of the sublime."—(Schopenhauer, "World as Will and Idea." Book III., p. 265.)

"If we turn our glance to those who have overcome the world : then instead of the restless striving and effort, instead of the constant transition from wish to fruition and from joy to sorrow, instead of the never-satisfied and never-dying hope which constitutes the life of the man who wills, we shall see that peace which is above all reason, that perfect calm of the spirit, that deep rest, that inviolable calm and serenity, the mere reflection of which in the countenance, as Raphael and Correggio have represented it, is an entire and certain gospel ; *only knowledge remains*, the will has vanished."— ("World as Will and Idea." Book IV., p. 531.) "We freely acknowledge that what remains after the entire abolition of will is *for those who are still full of will*, certainly nothing ; but, conversely, to those in whom the will has turned and denied itself, *this our world*, which is so real, with all its suns and milky ways—is nothing."—("World as Will and Idea." Book IV., p. 532.) "Death is like the setting of the sun, which is only apparently swallowed up by the night, but in reality, itself the source of all light, burns without intermission, brings new days to new worlds, is always rising and setting."—("World as Will and Idea." Book IV., p. 473.)

"If we lose ourselves in the contemplation of the infinite greatness of the universe in space and time, meditate on the thousands of years that are past or to come, or if the heavens at night actually bring before our eyes innumerable worlds, and so force upon our consciousness the immensity of the universe, we feel ourselves dwindle to nothing ; as individuals, as living bodies, as transient phenomena of will, we feel ourselves pass away and vanish into nothing like drops in the ocean. But at once there rises against this ghost of our own nothingness, against such *lying impossibility*, the immediate consciousness that all these worlds exist only as our idea, only as modifications of the *eternal subject of pure knowing, which we find ourselves to be* as soon as we forget our individuality. The vastness of the world rests now in us, we are one with the world, and therefore not oppressed, but exalted by its immensity. It is the transcending of our own individuality, the sense of the sublime."—("World as Will and Idea." Book III., p. 266.)

NOTE XXIV.—"*All lines of true human thought focus in religion.*"
"*My thoughts upon these matters came to me as creative artist in my intercourse with the public.*"—(P. 55.)

"Man was constituted for a time only in this world, that he might ascend from the inferior things, and seek after the superior things ; that is, that by natural light and wisdom, as it were from a looking-glass or shadow, he might learn to know and apprehend the heavenly Light, and Wisdom, at whose majesty and glory, all natural things, although glorious, might plainly vanish and be annihilated ; and so, leaving the inferior and lesser light, he should suddenly betake himself to and follow the greater and superior Light : *But these things are not propounded and written to that end that they should happen in contempt of philosophy, or of natural sciences, arts, and faculties,* which are and flourish among men, and which in this life cannot but be ; *but rather that we, being fraught with the sagacity of the Light of Nature, may be led further, may go forward and be excited to the knowledge of the greater Light,* which may confer upon us a new birth, eternal life and salvation."—(Astrologie Theologized, 1649.)

We read in Deuteronomy: " My doctrine shall drop as the rain, my speech shall distill as the dew, or be as the small dew upon the tender herb and as the showers upon the grass " ; and in the Gospel according to St. John: "If any man thirst let him come unto me and drink." Hence, according to the symbolism of the Scriptures, water, in the good sense, signifies divine truth in the Holy Word, and in the Human Mind. But in its opposite sense, water signifies man's self-derived intelligence and fleshly or physical wisdom. By the fishes of the sea are signified all the principles of scientific truth ; thus in the Book of Revelations, John hears every creature that was in the sea praising the Lord. Hence, the curious miracle of the piece of money in the mouth of the fish is interpreted thus : " The Divine command to Peter, ' Go to the sea and cast a hook,' meant ' Go and investigate the inner principles of the sciences, and every one of them will be found to contain within itself the tribute which it owes to spiritual religion, and which it cheerfully renders up.' The Lord said to Peter, ' Take up the fish that first cometh up, and thou shalt find a piece of money,' to instruct us that every science, no matter what, contains its own tribute, which it pays at the shrine of religion. Every fish when its mouth is opened, every science when its interior principles are explored by Peter, or those grounded in a pure faith, will be found to contain the tribute money. When this is discovered and demanded for the interests of true religion, it is instantly yielded up. These sciences, when internally explored, will be found to contain infallible proofs of the existence of a Supreme Being, pointing at the same time to the spirituality and superiority of religion, which they constantly serve, and to which they are tributary." (See " The Science of Scriptural Correspondences Elucidated," by Madely and Barrett.) " The present growing discord between the TREMENDOUS EMPIRE OF THE SENSES and the SOLITARY SUPREMACY OF THE SOUL must be resolved. Hitherto, churches, whether Catholic or Protestant, have dealt with the Senses separately by crushing them, and with the Soul separately by isolating it ; but Asceticism and Mysticism combined have failed altogether to grapple with the whole truth of life, to *place* the Senses, to *make room* for the various noble activities and desirable pursuits which, in many ways not essentially religious, make life worth living. . . . The Christianity of the Future . . . will recognize that some are born to be Reservoirs of spiritual power for the world, as others are born to be Reservoirs of political, poetic, industrial, artistic, or scientific power for the world. . . . The notion that Felix Mendelssohn would have been better occupied in preaching the Gospel than in composing music, or that Charles Dickens would have been better employed as a missionary than in writing books, is plainly erroneous. The Christian Church (although it began with such-like teaching in a season of protest and reaction) has long since practically abandoned it in detail ; but the Christian Church has *never changed its theory—it has never re-stated its relations with the world, although the world has entirely changed its relations with the Church.* The Christianity of the future must set itself to solve this problem. You may say it has been practically solved by a thousand noble lives. So it has ; but not by our Christianity. . . . The Christianity of the Future, whilst proclaiming with the voice of an archangel the SOLITARY SUPREMACY OF THE SOUL, the majesty of the higher intuitions, man's spiritual affinity with God, and the paramount duty of aiming at a moral harmony here as the prelude to a blessed immortality, must recognize as on a parallel, but not antagonistic, plane, the EMPIRE OF THE SENSES, the claims of the outward and visible world, and the divinity of secular knowledge. Christianity must learn what the religion of Jesus is, after all, best fitted to teach—that what God has permitted to be true in the world of Nature cannot really be opposed to any religious truth. She must fit in science ; she must re-state her theological conceptions until they are brought into some sort of harmony with that state of progress which God has permitted the human mind to reach. . . . Jesus is the Soul-master, not the School-master ; but those ministers and stewards of the mysteries who teach in His name, are bound to place us in right relations with the constitution of human nature and all the permanent facts of life, and neither to ignore them, violate them, nor denounce them. . . . If the Religion of Jesus is, as so many of us feel and believe it to be, the Religion of Humanity and the Hope of the Future, it will be able to deal with the world 'and all its lights and shadows, all the weal and all the woe' ; it will have the courage at due seasons to come out of the cloister and throw off the cowl ; it will know how to rejoice with them that do rejoice as well as to weep with those that weep ; it will not only burn up wickedness and warm our congealed life of selfishness with Philanthropy, but it will glow with the painter's colors, thrill with the musician's harmonies, brighten with the wreathed smiles of women and children ; . . . and yet, beyond all these, be full also of the things which eye hath not seen nor ear heard." ("The Conquering Cross" : Rev. H. A. Haweis, M.A.)

" Man has instinctively felt, in all times and under all religions, that he must look to Art to express and interpret the feelings into which Science and Philosophy and Ethics lead him, and to form for him a worship for the Infinite Truth and Beauty and Goodness.   Thus, the architect has reared the massive temple and the beautiful minster ; and the sculptor has adorned them with the noblest figures of saints and heroes, with dim visions of angels stooping from the shadowed niches in the walls ; and the painter has lifted above the altar the seraphic form of the Mother and the Child ; through the rich rose-window the golden light streaming in upon the fretted vault and long-drawn nave and shadowy aisle on the choicest symbols which man has fashioned through the ages wherewith to express his awe and reverence, his thought and feeling before the Infinite Mystery ; while the music of the masters filled the vast building with tumultuous waves of sound, thrilling the soul with joy unspeakable and full of glory, whispering secrets of peace to hearts bowed down with woe, bearing within souls tempted and tried the echoes of that voice heard of old—" Come unto me, all ye that labor and are heavy laden, and I will give you rest."   All this has been right.   If worship is the highest act of man, it demands for its rightful rendering the highest powers of man.   Whatever can be brought into the service of the church, wherewith to express its faith and hope and charity, is legitimate.   It needs no apology.   It vindicates its place by appealing to the mind and heart and conscience of men.   Our worship ought to be just as noble and dignified and beautiful and rich as it is possible for us to make it, so long as it is charged with true thought and pure feeling, so long as it is an uplift of the soul. *The moment that the symbol obscures the reality ; that the music tickles the ear and starts the feet to the measures of the dance, instead of breathing upon the soul and stirring the wings of aspiration ; that the picture above the altar arrests the mind as well as the eye, and one stops with thinking about it, instead of through it feeling its way into that which it signs in form and color ;* that the things round about the altar absorb the attention of the worshippers, and in their due arrangement the sense of worship is discharged—*that moment the presence of art is an impertinence, and being an impertinence becomes a blasphemy.*   Then the stern, grim Puritan needs to enter our temple, hew down our statues, tear our pictures from the walls, white-wash the frescos stained in the plaster, strip the altar, rear the table again, banish the choir and the organ, and bring us back to the stern simplicity of mind and conscience in which we worship that God who is spirit in spirit and in truth. But surely, friends, it is possible for us now at length to be Catholics in all rightful emphasis of the imagination, and yet to be Protestants in all rightful emphasis of the reason and conscience ; and *in worship as in life to declare—That which God has joined together, let no man put asunder.*   Only let us be on our guard.   The more dignified and noble we seek to make our worship, through the ministry of art, the more let us remember the great saying of Confucius : ' If my soul is not engaged in high worship, it is even as though I worshipped not.' "—(Rev. R. Heber Newton, D.D.)

NOTE XXV.—" *True art found to be at one with religion.*"—(P. 55.)

" One might affirm that when Religion becomes artificial, it is reserved for art to rescue the kernel of Religion by taking the mythical symbols which artificial Religion would have accepted as literally true, and instead interpreting them according to their symbolical worth, thus enabling us, by means of an ideal representation of those symbols, to discern the deep truth concealed within them. Religion becomes wholly artificial when it is forced to a continual extension of dogmatic symbols, for the sole true and divine contents are thus buried beneath an increasing accumulation of things incredible which are recommended for belief. It is with a feeling of this truth that Religion has always sought the aid of art : while art in turn fulfills her true mission only when, by ideal representations of an allegoric type, she conduces to the apprehension of the inner kernel of Religion, the inexpressible Divine Truth."—(Wagner, 1880, p. 269.)

NOTE XXVI.—" *Only through error can we poor earthworms get to a knowledge of the truth.*"—(P. 55.)

" Thus have we, as closely and perhaps as satisfactorily as, in such circumstances, might be, followed Teufelsdröckh through the various successive states and stages of Growth, Entanglement, Unbelief, and almost Reprobation, into a certain clearer state of what he himself seems to consider as Conversion. ' Blame not the word,' says he ; ' rejoice rather that such a word, signifying such a thing, has come to light in our Modern Era, though hidden from the wisest Ancients. The Old World knew nothing of Conversion : instead of an *Ecce Homo,* they had only some *Choice of Hercules.* It was a new-attained progress in the Moral Development of Man : hereby has the Highest come home to the bosoms of the most Limited ; what to Plato was but a hallucination, and to Socrates a chimera, is now clear and certain to your Zinzendorfs, your Wesleys, and the poorest of their Pietists and Methodists.'

" It is here, then, that the spiritual majority of Teufelsdröckh commences : we are henceforth to see him ' work in well-doing,' with the spirit and clear aims of a Man."—(" Sartor Resartus" : Carlyle.)

NOTE XXVII.—" *The name for the ' Victory, or the most Perfect Salvation' was found. It was Parsifal.*"—(P. 57.)

" A great many people were against Wagner's great semi-sacred musical drama called ' Parsifal ' till they saw and heard it. The glamour of mediæval fantasy and Catholic legend just saved it from open denunciation, but we can all remember the doubtful shudder which ran through some art circles, as a rule not over-squeamish, and all religious coteries, when it was proposed to put the Lord's Last Supper on the stage ! True, ' Parsifal ' does not quite do that, but it is next door to it. The associations are there, the function is there, the communicants are there, even the scenic suggestion of our Lord Himself is there, and an incident in His life finds expression in the person of Parsifal and the woman Kundry, who, in the hour of her penitence, bathes his feet with her tears, and wipes them with the hair of her head ; and yet no one who has seen ' Parsifal ' comes away without the most reverent sympathy for this ideal representation of all that was most pure and elevating in mediæval Roman Catholicism.

" Once more I seem to be at Bayreuth when first that stage drama unrolled itself before the eyes of the pilgrims assembled in the dim musical sanctuary, for such it was to us. We were all silent ; nothing moved ; nothing was visible, save an eager mist of faces half seen in the weird light reflected from the illuminated stage, and the great parables of life and death, of frailty and sanctification, the spiritual secrets of time and eternity, unrolled themselves before us, august revelations of the soul, convincing the world of judgment and of righteousness and of sin. Yes, there was the terrible struggle between the flesh and the spirit in Kundry's own double nature ; there was the dread but triumphant passage from innocent ignorance to the knowledge of good and evil in the victorious guileless One. There was the love that had power to pardon, because it had been tempted without sin. Was ever, in all art creation, balm for the broken spirit and the contrite heart like the tender benison of that Good-Friday music which comes with the weeping of the penitent woman and the waving of the hands that blessed ? But who can tell of the songs of the angels far above the high dome of Montsalvat, what time the knights of the Sangrail are met in holy conclave to celebrate their love-feast ?

" The pain of the crucifixion has long passed. The agony of the ' Beloved ' has become a memory and a faith, enshrined in celestial peace and glory ; it all seems to visit earth for a moment to hallow, to feed, to lift up the faithful, as the Grail passes, buoyed up on the ocean of strange sound, and smitten with supernal light, ' rose-red with beatings in it.'

" I shall never forget the indescribable emotion which seized the whole assembly on the first representation of that daring and unparalleled scene. The knights seated in semicircle, with golden goblets before them, in the halls of Montsalvat. The faint plash of distant fountains adown the marble corridor is heard. Amfortas rises pale with pain and torn by remorse, yet holding on high the crystal goblet. The light fades out of the golden dome, a holy twilight falls, and strange melodies float down from above, till, in the deepening gloom, the goblet slowly glows and reddens like a ruby flame, and the knights fall prostrate in an ecstasy of devotion ; a moment only, the crimson fades out, the crystal is dark, the Grail has passed. I looked round upon the silent audience whilst this astonishing celebration was taking place. The whole assembly was motionless ; all seemed to be solemnized by the august spectacle—seemed almost to share in the devout contemplation and trance-like worship of the holy knights. Every thought of the stage had vanished. Nothing was further from my own thoughts than play-acting. I was sitting in devout and rapt contemplation. Before my eyes had passed a symbolic vision of prayer and ecstasy, flooding the soul with overpowering thoughts of the divine sacrifice and the mystery of unfathomable love.

" The people seemed spellbound. Some wept, some gazed entranced with wide-open eyes, some heads were bowed as in prayer."—(Rev. H. A. Haweis, M.A.)

THE END.

www.ingramcontent.com/pod-product-compliance
Lightning Source LLC
Chambersburg PA
CBHW032146010726
47493CB00008BA/2609